# 3 NATIONS ANTHOLOGY

D1417936

# 3 Nations Anthology
## Native, Canadian & New England Writers

Edited by Valerie Lawson

Resolute Bear Press
ROBBINSTON, MAINE

Published by Resolute Bear Press

Works in this anthology have previously appeared in:

"**Terminal Moraine**" by Leonore Hildebrandt, *Café Review,* Vol. 26, Winter 2015

"**Water/Nebi**" by Cheryl Savageau, *Yellow Medicine Review*, Fall 2012

"**Wait Five Minutes**" by Karen Skolfield, *Zone 3*

"**Tribal/State Relations in the State of Maine USA**" by Donna Loring, *Portland Press Herald/Maine Sunday Telegram*

"**Heirloom**" by Karen Skolfield, *MIRAMAR*

"**How a Community of Women**" by Cindy Veach, *Sou'wester*

"**Waverly and the C-Notes**" by Frederick Lowe, *Contemporary Haibun Online*, Vol. 12, No. 3, October 2016

"**Thinking Potatoes**" by Leonore Hildebrandt, *Otis Nebula* 10, Fall 2015

"**Three Deer in Oquossoc**" by Sonja Johanson, *Plum Tree Tavern*

"**Observations on the Garden, Fourth of July**" by Dennis Camire, *Combed by Crows* (Deerbrook Editions)

"**Lost and Found Logs**" by Charles McGowan, *Cross Border Tales, Maine, New Brunswick, and More*

"**Chance of Afternoon Showers**" by JD Rule will appear in the novel, *Buster Lomen*, in the summer of 2017.


Cover Art: "**Home**" by Valerie Lawson, Digital Collage


3 Nations Anthology/ edited by Valerie Lawson.
ISBN 978-0-9988195-1-8

Resolute Bear Press
PO Box 14
1175 US Route 1
Robbinston, ME 04671

# Contents

## This That This

Listen: Before iron, before The Cross and The Book. Before masts. This black stone sluiced with fog. A whale sleeping.

In the black bowl, where the stars live, deer, wolf, rabbit whorl with the hunter until first light walks the tide. Insinuates through fog. Traces beach rock. Sweeps this black, glistening stone. A whale sleeping.

First light warms this hand that pecks and carves this story. How deer and bear fell into the arms of earth. How the people ate until they were ready to sing.

This is a story. Many people dancing. This story has a song. Has smoke rising, clarifying spruce and pine. This is not a dream. Stone claps stone. This is a story of arrival and going back. Of deer and bear falling to earth. Of masts.

Before iron. Stone claps stone, a declaration into this black rock.

—Elizabeth Sprague

Super moon, rising
over lichen-swathed headstones,
faces down the sun.

—Danielle Woerner

## Acadian Archaeology
*for Flannery*

I


My daughter digs
to claim the past for her Papa and me,
to know why we bow our heads,
to know why we look heavenward.
She shows us where pasts were buried:
the broken pottery,
the tarnished and twisted spoon,
the rusted flintlock
that whisper the past,
that claim we lived here and were
busy with that living when they
sent us away,
bound to return,
        to reclaim
                our language,
                our farms,
                our wives, husbands, and children,
                our God, Savior, and Mother,
                ourselves.


II


"You're walking on Acadian graves," my daughter said,
so we walked on, looking straight ahead.

"Look above, in the tree, an eagle's nest,"
so we looked heavenward.

"Here is where we dug,"
so we looked down.

Up the steps and into the chapel.
Like the stations of the cross, we visited each painting,

following the farmers to exile:
the reds of coats and flames,
the browns of soil and despair.

We looked to Mary, mistaken for Evangeline,
but Mary for the right bare foot,
Mary of the star on the flag.
Below her a list of names and I found ours.

We are included.
We are named.
We are Surette.
We are Acadians.

*Nous sommes Surette.*
*Nous sommes Acadiens.*

III

We were not allowed
to visit the Expulsion Cross.
The guide said
we would be risking our lives.

IV
It's not a name that
steps lightly off the tongue.
It more often trips among
the crack of Irish,

the music of Italian.
It's the other side of the family:
Farmers and fishermen,
Uncle Joe the oilman and Uncle Clarence the rope maker.
Dark and dull.
Homely and short.
Adults and children dressed in drab.
But here,
everyone is or has an
uncle, aunt, grandmother who is.
It marks each gravestone and mailbox.
It's emblazoned on softball jerseys.
It's Marie Babin's taken name,
trying to outlive them all
(like my Nana, 100 years old)
still alive on the ghostly white tablet
outside St. Joseph's church.
So I say it now a little more French.
I say it without embarrassment.
I say it like it has meaning
as I cross the bridge
over dangerous waters
and drive the half moon
of Surette's Island, Nova Scotia.

—David R. Surrette

## Terminal Moraine

I worry about gutters,
the washed-out road, corroded pipes.
And squirrels—they are everywhere—
on edge, just like me.

"Go home," I yell at the neighbor's dogs.
Naked-pink, they scramble into the woods.

And what is wild about berry-fields?
My friend and I walk the barrens—
the eskers and kettle holes
look different—almost rearranged—

with the sweep of new roads, piled
rock, machinery and warning signs.

My neighbor breeds the dogs
in kennels—all day they yip and wail.
Finally the plumber shows up,
tells me about his blocked arteries.

Landforms can be read, flow rates measured.
Go touch the wind to see how it blows.

—Leonore Hildebrandt

# The Green Quilt

Cheryl Savageau

The palette is mostly grey-greens and browns, very subdued, with some turquoise, gold, orange and mauve. The woods on an overcast day, instead of bright sun. Colors that disappear.

I am working in layers, cutting things off, appliquéing over what I don't like. I add a diagonal strip of rocks for tension, a small piece of light turquoise with wisps of cloud, and there's water in a block. Later I will add small pieces over the whole quilt, like confetti, to hold it together. I'm trying to keep in mind that this initial piecing doesn't have to be the total result, but rather is a base to be over-laid.

The blocks have become mini-landscapes, the layering of fabrics like the layers of the woods. I want people to feel as if they can walk into each block. These totally free-pieced blocks have houses, rivers, chimneys—some of it intentional, but some came serendipitously, appearing as if by magic.

I add darker stone walls, sew diagonal strips across several blocks. The stone walls, broken and meandering, and the darkness of the stone, in contrast to the lighter stonework in some of the blocks makes them seem damp. I like the way the eye follows the stone wall, or the water, and stops at individual trees or houses or other spots, then moves on.

The clumps of birches are mostly appliqué, but one is pieced into the block. I use a black and silver metallic and sew a blanket stitch with fairly wide stitches to mimic the bark markings. I add another clump for balance and because the log cabin block is too dark and overbearing. The golden river birches lighten it up.

I have to rip out the satin stitch on the tiny triangular appliqué. The center block I was having trouble with is now in the upper right corner—it was too subdued for the center but works well as a corner block. The center block pulls you in, like an opening in the trees.

I am starting to see how to put the whole thing together, using some straight edges, but keeping the free quality of the irregular blocks. I attach some pieces of stone wall with safety pins. The illusion of ownership.

# Borderline

Stephanie S. Gough

There was a time when I was the only one in my family who was not American.

An international border has been the defining line in my life, surpassing the importance of all other lines, between strength and weakness, ego and superego, love and hate, success and failure, birth and death. I have played with it, learned to smuggle over it, jumped back and forth it like a skipping rope, been restrained by it and freed by it.

I am from a Canadian island, population 900, connected to the mainland solely by bridge to the United States, banked on both ends by border checkpoints. The story goes the man tasked with drafting the boundary for this region was drunk the night his unsteady hand forever cast our lot in with Canada.

We are tiny, but we are international. We are Canadian (not really). We are Americans, until turned back at the border. We are both and neither. We redefine national attachment. Not tied to nationhood, we cling to island. We admit nationality according to what suits us best on a given occasion, or at least it used to be that way. Are we then, have we been, the world's first truly global citizens? I believe we are in the running.

My grandmothers grew up in Maine, my grandfathers in Canada. My father was born in the United States. My mother in Saint John, New Brunswick. My siblings were born one in Canada and two in America. Half my extended family live spread across the United States. A smattering has taken up residence in chilly Ottawa, or Toronto, or Nova Scotia.

When I want to go to a bar, I cross a border. For many years, I could only buy groceries if I left my country, and still today, I can only gas up that way. I have loved fiercely over that line. My best friend lives in a different time zone, two miles from my house. When I was a teenager, my first lover crossed that line on foot to visit me. Around here, we marry across that line, the trunks of our cars are loaded with potluck treats for a baby shower, a church supper, weddings, gifts are carted back and forth. It matters not to us, but every day we wonder if this will be the day we are caught doing something illegal.

When I was very little, I thought Duty was a woman my parents had to pay when we came home. I imagined her with a beehive. I must have been at least five years old the day we crossed without pulling in and I asked indignantly, "Aren't you going to pay her?" I can see the baffled looks on my parents' faces now as they turned to look at me in the back of the car, and chimed in puzzled unison, "Who?"

Some years you were not allowed to bring citrus fruit across. Others it was potatoes. Some years you could bring six beer with you, others none, and still others it depended on how long you had been out. Sometimes you could bring $20 (CDN, not USD) worth of groceries with you, receipts in sweaty palm as you drove up to the window. Some years, it didn't really matter. I have often worn four layers of clothing through customs, normally just before Christmas or the start of a new school year. By the age of 10, I knew all the best hiding places in a car: under the dash, in the spare wheel, under the hood, back seat consoles. Phrases like "out on a 48" were normal lingo. In the years when restrictions were especially tight, Santa often brought his gifts by outboard on dark, snowy nights.

Here, we grow up in the shadow of a great American president. A third of our territory (9 miles by 3 miles, or 14.4km by 4km) is comprised of the only fully international park in the world, jointly funded by the Canadian and US governments and staffed equally by folks from both sides. Half-hearted attempts to stir Canadian patriotism in the national K–12 curriculum on the island are met with blank stares from the children. Our kids know I-95, Bangor, Florida. They play basketball on both sides of the border. But, at the same time, a part of us clings to Canada. We agree with universal healthcare, socialism, well-paid teachers. We don't mind the taxes, but we like to smuggle our alcohol just the same.

9

I have spent half my life filing immigration papers, all the while separated from my future, my family, my history by that dividing line, or so I thought. American rights, Canadian rights, green cards, nationalization, *jus sanguinis*, deciphering convoluted immigration laws (some of the densest in US history were those in place during the last century) that changed with each generation—all just run-of-the-mill stuff around here.

I don't know who the first boat baby was, but before the bridge was built in the 60s, there were many born as their mothers were frantically rowed across the Narrows, en route to hospital. The nebulous nationalities of these babies born in international waters was somehow assumed by us all. A certain vagueness surrounded our identities, accompanied by a gentle evasion of pointed questioning, a scuffle of the feet, a slight aversion of the eye. We were the grey zone, and we embraced it wholeheartedly. Yes! I am American. Yes! I am Canadian—said by rote for so long, in the end nobody really knew the truth, even about themselves.

In 2009, an event took place that changed our relationship with that blurred line. It was a ripple that had been coming since 2001, but its arrival still came as a shock to islanders: The Western Hemisphere Travel Initiative. The sudden requirement of passports for border crossings between the United States and Canada sent us into a frantic scurry. We were forced to determine our own nationalities. Some of us were forced to choose. When the dust had settled, I had joined the ranks of dual citizens in my family. As for the rest, they probably chose what suited them best at the time.

In the end, it really didn't change things. Was I more American with my new passport in hand? Not at all, as it turned out. Did I feel a renewed affinity with my Canadian roots then? Can't say I did. It seemed nothing could change how we felt deep down inside, nor who we were, at least in our own minds, and in that, there was a lasting message for anybody who cared to take notice.

Don't try to define us. We have done so already. We are Campobello'ers.

# Chance of Afternoon Showers

## JD Rule

This storm was a bit more than the weather service called for, at least early on. The forecaster out on Nova Scotia—the slightly wacky one—he was the one that predicted this was coming four days before it hit.

But now, after three days, it had started to get to folks. You could tell by the way they'd duck into the hardware store or the grocery, jacket pulled tight and head down, forgetting about the usual cheery greeting. When the wind takes people's breath away, they get edgy.

A Nor'easter can do that, with the gusts often topping sixty and occasionally a lot more, bringing trees down and worse. Six inches of rain over forty-eight hours didn't make it any easier, but at least it wasn't cold. Last time it blew like this, the big church on the hill lost a century-old stained glass window.

On my way over to the waterfront I spotted Jake coming out of the hardware store and invited him into my car, out of the downpour. A good crowd had gathered in the wharf parking lot, watching the chaotic waters and the boats struggling in the four and five foot waves. When the wind howls down the St. Croix River and the Western Passage, Eastport provides little shelter and the twenty-mile fetch means the seas rise tall. Even Dudley Island provides scant defense from the northern winds.

But the wind-driven waves are only part of the story.

With the usual twenty-foot tides, the current flow is both predictable and inexorable. When a four-knot current flows ninety degrees off the wind, the boats are forced to face the seas broadside, wallowing dangerously as each trough is followed by a windblown crest. A lobsterman, lacking the top-hamper of a dragger, has a better chance, but only marginally. A boat that faces the wind head-on can stand up to nearly anything—not so when it stands sideways or stern-to. When this happens during winter conditions, ice build-up has sunk more than one vessel, going down right at its mooring.

This morning there would be no ice, but there were several fishermen prepared to put skiffs in the water if their boat looked like it was in danger of foundering. "Guys have died trying that," Jake muttered as we watched out of the car window. It didn't look like any of the men on the wharf were about to defy the storm, but desperation makes for tough decisions. Every fisherman is a gambler.

Jake's boat, *Three Nine's Fine*, was riding okay, and a little closer in Buster's *Lobster One* appeared to be holding its own. Maybe that was just the luck of the draw, plus they were both rigged for pulling lobster traps.

A hard gust rocked the car, shaking us like we would be blown against the hillside behind the wharf parking area, and a torrent of rain partially obscured our vision. Out in front, *Rogue Wave*, a forty-two-foot dragger loaded down with an urchin dredge and a tall rig took a wave over the starboard rail, momentarily swamping the deck. It wallowed and staggered and the blast rolled it hard onto the port side beam ends, reducing the freeboard to zero. I held my breath for a near-eternity before the antenna began to climb back towards the sky and a waterfall gushed out of the scuppers. When it finally lurched back to near-vertical, she rode noticeably lower and a half-inch stream of water appeared, flowing out of a fitting on the port side.

"Shit!" Jake muttered. "Bill Andrews' boat. He done got his cabin flooded. Musta stove in the companionway boards." He shook his head. "Pumps gonna take forever ta' clear that." Several men rushed to the point on the shore closest to the stricken boat and stood, gesticulating against the howling wind. *Rogue Wave* was now riding bow down, tugging hard against the rode like it wanted to rip the mooring out of the bottom. "He's with his wife in Bangor. She's in the hospital." He stared out of the windshield. "That's why he didn't pull that friggin' dredge off," he grumbled as if talking to himself. The stream of water pumping out of the side looked puny in the gale, like a crewman pissing against the tide.

Another large wave bore down on the boat, this time crashing over the bow. A foot of green water swept across the wheelhouse roof and poured onto the deck, but this time the scuppers kept up, at least mostly.

Buster drove onto the wharf, towing a skiff. "He's not going out there," I blurted out in horror. "Is he?"

"Not without me, he ain't." Jake put his shoulder against the wind to shove the car door open and dashed across the parking lot, head down. Several men helped the two wrestle a pump out of the back of Buster's truck into the skiff, then he backed the trailer down the kelp-strewn ramp. When he jumped out another took his place behind the wheel. The skiff was floated off with Jake holding the pump and Buster lowering the outboard into place while the truck raced back up the ramp, leaving them to confront the tempest alone. By this time, I was on the edge of the parking lot, standing with a small crowd.

Within a long couple of minutes the skiff was tied alongside *Rogue Wave*. Jake clambered on board then leaned over the side to grab ahold of the pump, seemingly ignoring the wildly pitching deck that threatened to hurl him overboard with every lurch. A chain swung drunkenly, hanging down from the rig, but he paid it no heed. The skiff tipped up on one side like a sudden gust would flip it but Buster continued to hoist the pump up and over the rail, pushing while Jake pulled, then dragged himself on board. As soon as his weight was off the skiff, a gust picked it up and it slid under a wave.

A minute later a large hose was hanging over the starboard side, next to the wheel. We stood helplessly watching while sheets of rain slanted across the wharf and the waves crashed against the rip-rap, sending salt spray into the howling winds. It was not possible to stay dry and none of us tried.

We all cheered when the four-inch stream started flowing fast and heavy, but at this point the skiff was flooded. Obviously, the pump had been started without incident, but the sound was carried off by the wind. When Jake waved, we barely made out he was holding a microphone. One of the men on the shore grabbed a hand-held from his pickup.

"Hey Cap'n," the man next to me said into the radio. "You guys havin' fun out there?"

"Jist hunky-dory." Jake's voice was scratchy and the wind got into the mike and the pump engine droned loudly, but he was still clearly audible. "Got 'nuff stuff out here, we're fixin' this busted board," he radioed back. "But maybe we gonna need us a lift." The only thing still visible of Buster's skiff was the top of the outboard and while the storm raged there was little hope of getting it refloated and the engine started. Two men backed a truck with another skiff to the top of the ramp.

"All set," the man radioed back. "You just say when." By this time *Rogue Wave* was riding noticeably higher in the bow and not pulling quite as hard.

A man I had spoken with occasionally in the bar said to me, "Them guys out there, they use'ta be partners." He pointed at *Lobster One.*

"Partners?" Nobody'd mentioned this story to me, at least not before now. "What happened?"

The man shrugged. "Buster done bought out his share." He turned back towards the bay where gobs of frothy foam continued to blow off the wave tops.

Jake's voice crackled over the radio again. "Bill's got himself a cribbage board out here. Buster and me, we gonna play us a match."

The reply was immediate. "We be ready with yer ride when you need it, Cap'n."

"Hey," Jake radioed back. "How long ta' high water?"

"Nother hour."

"So this friggin' current's gonna change right soon."

"Already started to."

"You see Bill Andrews," Jake's voice crackled across the airwaves, "you tell him he owes us a beer."

## A Lake in the Woods

A cloud. A lake. What do you want? A gazebo?
I won't have it. The odor of new cut wood
mingles with rising steam from a silver tea-ball
I steep for my next-door neighbor who's no good

at anything but literature, though he sits
and dawdles over a cup of herbal tea
all decked out in his big-game hunter's kit—
a blank-verse epic poem in camouflage motley—

and grumbles away about the Republican lock
on local politics, while an election unrolls
somewhere beyond our horizon, there where smoke
lifts the sky on its shoulders over the hill.

I'm restless. I've been tired of nodding my head
for twenty minutes now. Out on the water
there's something doing something I don't understand—
maybe a tumbling log, or maybe an otter,

So there you are, that's what my life is like.
Take it or leave it. A cloud. A bore. A lake.

—J. Kates

15

# Water/Nebi

*… this is the river I belong to…*

Polin, Abenaki leader 1739


We breathe
the traveling clouds
and drink what falls
glistening from cliffs
and into whirlpool
basins carved in granite
on its way back to sky

water me
glisten me
carve and
whirlpool me
cascade me
white water me
sing me babble me
pool me pond me
swamp me
bog me
trout and salmon me
frog and dragonfly me
loon and otter me

breathe me
the humid sky
while leaves
gather pools
of summer air

*Nebi* we say
*wligonebi*
the water is good

—Cheryl Savageau

## Wait Five Minutes

I duck into the Visitor's Center and shake the water off my jacket. The woman behind the desk asks if the rain's stopped. When I say not yet, she says if you don't like the weather here, just wait five minutes. Well isn't that true, I reply. What I like about the five-minute statement is that it's always said with the air of a grand but knowable secret being given away. It takes both people speaking their lines, nodding and smiling at just the right times. I like the predictability of it, and when someone says it to me, which is often, I play right along as if it were new and wondrous, a thing to be turned over and over. Sometimes I'm even the one to start it, and the other person will look at me with an air of gratitude and say, well isn't that true. How much fonder could I get of humanity? In New England, it's as close as we get to hugging. Another batch of visitors comes in and I can feel my heart swell. Soon enough we'll greet each other. Outside the rain goes on and on.

—Karen Skolfield

# Tribal/State Relations in the State of Maine USA

Donna M. Loring

"Circle the wagons!" is a phrase I learned watching the old western movies on TV when I was a kid. It was done to protect the white people—who were moving west (to steal Indian land)—from those vicious savages. The savages were to be eliminated in any way possible because they were an impediment to white progress. No thought was given to the fact that the Indian people were actual human beings with families and a need to preserve their own way of life.

On May 19th, 2015, I listened to the Judiciary Public hearing on five Indian bills.

- **L.D. 239,** a proposal to create a permanent Wabanaki law enforcement seat on the board of the Maine Criminal Justice Academy.
- **L.D. 267,** a proposal to implement the recommendations of the Maine-Wabanaki State Child Welfare Truth and Reconciliation Commission.
- **L.D. 268,** a proposal to give tribal courts jurisdiction over cases involving Indian women who are physically abused by non-Indian men.
- **L.D. 893,** requiring the state to print the section of the state constitution outlining Maine's obligations toward Indian tribes under a 1794 treaty with Massachusetts.
- **L.D. 1094,** a proposal to recognize the governmental powers of the Passamaquoddy Tribe and Penobscot Nation.

The thought of "Circle the Wagons!" came to mind. The committee circled the wagons on every single bill. There was no way any of those Indian bills were going to make it through committee. I know this because I was a committee member representing the Penobscot nation for nine years. I know how things work.

The awful truth is these committee members see the Tribes as foreigners (A Nation within a Nation) or even just the enemy impeding the State's progress. They see us this way because they do not know any better. They are trying to do the right thing for the "Common Good" They were never educated in Tribal-State Relations. They know nothing about the Land Claims Settlement Act, and yet they are expected to make policy decisions on that document. It's like asking a carpenter to do heart surgery!

My thoughts went back to the "Circle the wagons!" cry. Two worlds collided back in those times and the Indian world, as we knew it was blown apart like so many little pieces of shattered glass. We have tried to piece those shards back together ever since. It is almost impossible to do when every tool we have is being taken away from us. I wondered if these committee members knew anything of the Tribes contribution to this State and our Country. The years of loyalty the Tribes had given them are extraordinary in and of themselves.

Martin Luther King Jr. wrote: "Our nation was born in genocide when it embraced the doctrine that the original American, the Indian, was an inferior race. Even before there were large numbers of Negroes on our shore, the scar of racial hatred had already disfigured colonial society. From the sixteenth century forward, blood flowed in battles over racial supremacy. We are perhaps the only nation which tried as a matter of national policy to wipe out its indigenous population. Moreover, we elevated that tragic experience into a noble crusade. Indeed, even today we have not permitted ourselves to reject or feel remorse for this shameful episode. Our literature, our films, our drama, our folklore all exalt it. Our children are still taught to respect the violence which reduced a red-skinned people of an earlier culture into a few fragmented groups herded into impoverished reservations."

Even given the legacy that Dr. King refers to, the sad facts are these: Despite the horrific treatment we have endured from the white majority culture over the centuries of genocidal polices we have never lost our love for this land or this Country. We have fought in every war this Country has been in and fought valiantly! Our patriotic record speaks for itself. Native American soldiers have fought to protect the rights and freedoms of every United States Citizen in this Country. We love this Country—it is ours and we are one with it. We've shed our blood for it and paid the ultimate price many times over—more so than any other race. Don't you ever forget it!

We are United States citizens, we are Maine citizens and yes, we are Tribal citizens. Maine Tribes are being kept in poverty by the ignorance of our policy makers in Augusta. They don't seem to want to learn about this relationship except via the Attorney General's Office, which has done everything in its power to isolate us from society.

We are not foreigners in our own land. We are not the enemy. Stop circling the wagons. We have earned our citizenship.

Reprinted with permission from the *Portland Press Herald/Maine Sunday Telegram*. Reproduction does not imply endorsement.

# A Forest Journey

Rowan Miller

My name is Moira Lloyd, I'm twenty years old, and a wannabe photographer. I have always lived within the walls of my imperial daughter of the woods, my home town, Fredericton, New Brunswick. I went on countless trips in the province, and far beyond from time to time. Until recently saw the world from the arrow slits and airplane windows of my high castle beyond the clouds. But last week I went out the front gates and looked around, I saw life and its shadow in a world I thought blasted and forever dead. Places I ruled off during innumerable visits prior I saw for the first time.

With camera in hand I went searching for an easy A on a photography project. I'd find a historical marker or two, somewhere just far enough away from Freddy so not to run the risk of doubling up with any of my classmates, get a good perspective shot or two, and call it a day. "Perspectives Warping Perceptions of Historical Significance" was the assignment title. A couple of simple camera tricks and I would be one step closer to a certificate in photography.

I pulled up the highway 8, north towards Stanley. It was about 3:30, in mid-November, I'd arrive just in time for the golden hour, with all its photographic largesse. "No one goes up there," was my only thought, my only inspiration for driving that monotonous road, blurry of all landmarks. Nothing to make the drive memorable, just cliff faces blown from intruding hills as the highway leapt northwards.

When I pulled off the highway, on to the river road into town, I was dumped on an incoherent mass of stop-gap repairs and botched re-pavements, all covering a chaotic patchwork of potholes ranging in size from bowling ball to bathtub. Possibly the part of the landscape I noticed most, its effects most immediately "moving."

I had been up that way many times before. To see friends, to go tubing, to take photos of the Nashwaak in all its autumn grandeur. Stanley is a tiny village on the edge of nowhere. I knew it had a cenotaph and a small memorial garden. Both having been vandalized and robbed of all plaques, bronze or otherwise, it would make for an eerie shoot.

I got my photos, in good light and all. Making my way back, I opted to take the older 620, not really wanting to relive the ugly travesty of the 8 and its trauma inducing access road. I crossed the Nashwaak, over a bridge from which I had taken countless "pretty" pictures. As I made my way up the hill, an orange glimmer caught my eye. Just the right moment from just the right angle, the sun beamed off the few intact window panes on a long decaying three-story house. Looking into its overgrown yard, a mass of bare bushes and drooping oaks, I saw what might have been an attempt at a fashionable middle class abode from somewhere in the depths of the Victorian era. I stopped. Setting up my tripod, I took lots of photos.

After several minutes hunched over my camera, a woman pushing an overly large toddler in a pram shouted out to me.

"Like taking pictures? You should go check out Graveyard Hill. There's some real sights for you"

"Big shots—we get quite a few photographers up there!"

Slightly annoyed at the thought this was well-travelled ground, I did recall seeing a sign for Graveyard Hill after I left the memorials. I soon found its meaning. There were two cemeteries, back to back, hugging the road and separated by a single line of trees. I could indeed get a good shot of the entire village and valley. I wandered through the graveyard for a moment afterwards, more out of ritual compulsion than anything else. Fullerton, Sommerville, Summerville, Rouselle, four names that cropped up in a dozen or more locations from the 19th century to the 21st. A few Hudsons and Hendersons. One Richard DeMerchant, dead at 38, 1964, with the epitaph, "He fought a good fight."

On a whim, I continued uphill. My parents would be annoyed. I would be late for dinner, but I had never been beyond here and I was curious. For all I knew it was just forest, a wilderness completely. My phone had no signal. I couldn't check GPS, but I just wanted to see, in the waning hours of daylight, what lay beyond my backyard northern frontier, or at least expand it by a mile or two.

Above the hill, I passed farms and more graveyards. Though the evening's gold was beginning to give way to twilight, I stopped at another cemetery. Surrounded on all sides by now-barren fields, its driveway was lined by maples on both sides arching upwards and over. So evenly spaced, they were clearly planted with much care. Their canopy formed an arch of dormant life, but they led the way to nothing but a vacant gravel lot, forty feet or so square. Much of the cemetery still shimmered with colour. The grass glowed a pale yellow; tombstones reflected the setting sun's final orange flares. Here on this dreary gravel pad there was just gray, shaded by the maples around it. Setting up my tripod in the quite dead centre, I rotated the camera ever so carefully. I would make a panorama, the world around me from this spot of apparent nothingness.

The cemetery sat on the edge of a little farming hamlet. North from here the road dipped down a dark hill into true forest with no fields beyond. As I pulled out, I saw a little man at the edge of this precipice. He stood hunched over, his huge beard obscuring much of his face. He held one arm out, thumb bent at an almost unnatural ninety degrees, hitchhiking into the darkness.

At the end of the cemetery drive, right led back home. With an urge I can't quite explain, I took a left towards him and civilization's precipice. As I approached, he grinned into the headlights. I flung the door open.

"Oh yeah!" he shouted, with a few glances sizing up my tiny blue car. "You're not from around here, no way! Even more sweet of you to stop then!"

He spoke in a thick Francophone accent that I had heard once in a school trip up into Madawaska County. With giant bushy eyebrows and sooty baseball cap, he looked like a character from some terrible American faux reality extravaganza, except with all cruelty removed, hard edges smoothed out, with a flicker of oddball intelligence in his bizarrely large eyes.

"What brings you up here then?"

"A photography project. Just looking for some pretty sites to take pictures of," I chuckled nervously. What in god's name was I doing here?

"Oh, that then!" He laughed, a kind of raspy roar. "You going north, I assume? Up where I live, Napadogan, looks like a whole lot of ruins! You might appreciate it if we get there on time!"

He beamed at me.

"Uh… sure. How far is it?"

"Oh, just ten minutes or so. Maybe a bit longer in this little car!" His sentence again was tied up by that raspy laugh.

The drive was closer to half an hour, following the just barely paved road through a procession of dark valleys. On both sides trees rose up, their topmost branches still slightly glowing.

He called himself Monclaude, a pet name coined by his wife who had died in a car accident some years before. He had been involved but didn't explain. Since then he hadn't trusted himself to drive so he was left to the vicissitudes of hitchhiking. "It can be great fun at times!" he shouted when I commented on how difficult it must be. He claimed to be a mill worker, at a Napadogan factory where he had lived his whole life. With the forest thicker than ever and without any hints of civilization, I had a hard time believing a mill was soon to appear. When it did I was astounded.

"Yeah, we make veneer here. You're surprised, most people are. If you think there is still time, the remains of the old Legion branch might be worth looking at if you still want to take pictures."

We went up a ragged hill, past a couple of burnt-out houses. The mill across the railroad tracks billowed steam into the darkening sky. A couple of newer small bungalows crowded the road. Still inhabited, their windows gleamed. But the ones we passed as we chugged up the hill were blackened with soot and stood empty. All these homes were grander. Though their interiors appeared gutted, their husks remained with ornamented cornices and elaborately fronted gables. I pulled over as the road finally became completely overgrown. Monclaude got out automatically, hunching his way along, urging me to follow. For a moment, I stood motionless, surveying the abandoned houses descending down the hill.

"Monclaude, what happened to all of these houses?" I counted five or six of them, all attempting an antiquated middle class respectability, as opposed to the very clearly proletarian dwellings below. They wouldn't have been out of place in downtown Fredericton.

"Oh, they belonged to the mill owner and his foremen, back when they still lived around us! When I was a boy, the owner would even let us have the occasional dance in his parlour." He pointed to the empty bay frames of the largest house, obscured by bushes and spindly trees "The bastard was just trying to stay all chummy while never giving a raise! Ha!"

Monclaude led me past the houses to the highest ruin. The path was once a paved road, but the cracks had sprung so many saplings and sprigs I could only just make it out. Monclaude rushed ahead, his crooked frame surprisingly agile. He stood above me on some sort of platform, which turned out to be a cement pad, as I trudged up the last of the trail which turned into brick steps.

"This is the old Legion branch!" Monclaude declared with what seemed like pride. "We once had two dozen veterans here, and four more who never came back from the war!"

"The war?" I still don't know why I asked.

"World War II," he said flatly, and continued romping around the ruin. "This spot is much to me!" he shouted, half laughing. "Take lots of photos, maybe you'll catch some of our ghosts!"

"I figure you'd have ghosts."

"Oh yes! There are quite a few, not bad ghosts, but guardians. One in particular." He walked over to a piece of a metal handrail, leaning on the side of a fractured wall. "Back in the sixties, or maybe fifties, a big man tore this from the ground, and swung it like a maniac. He was defending the Branch from a biker gang of all things! Just drunks! Ha!" Monclaude's face, alive with energy, fell slightly. "He died a couple years later, heart attack, but he fought a good fight. This is almost a monument."

"He fought a good fight," I said to myself, pondering. "Was his name Richard DeMerchant?"

Monclaude's bushy eyebrows rose again. "How did you know?"

"I found his grave earlier down in Stanley."

"Oh yes, I suppose he is down there. I should visit him sometime." He looked away again, towards the mill. "Moira, it has been a pleasure, but I must now be going." He came over and shook my hand. "Many thanks again for the lift. If you are ever here in Napadogan again, please pop in!" He stepped off the platform, already on his way down the path. "I live in that little yellow house beyond the mill. I don't know if you drink, but I brew my own wine. Come back in a few weeks and I'll give you a bottle in thanks." He was already halfway down the hill, his walk a swinging gait that threw his body back and forth as he disappeared.

I did take a few shots, though the light by this time was very low. They showed up blue and grey, the few burnt frame remains of the Legion post sticking up out of the foundation. I did get some eerie photos. I even found a broken pipe, forgotten there who knows how many decades prior.

I never did ask Monclaude exactly what happened to all of these buildings, or why the population dropped, despite the mill still operating.

Finally, I turned towards home. Back through Stanley I passed again over the Nashwaak and towards the 620. It was a calmer drive than the abusively barren 8.-

As I rose out of a dip I saw what looked to be a tiny chapel, like many I had seen and photographed in the past. It was empty, its interior torn asunder, just like all the houses. It was halfway demolished, only the outer shell remained. Night had fallen on my drive back and the moon had not yet risen. Only an orange streetlight provided a hideous, explosive glow. A huge bonfire had ripped through the chapel's interior. I took a few photos, capturing the church's mortal wound and desecrated innards.

I wept in the haunted shadow of the dying church, with its baptismal font strewn against a tree, the mouldings once so lovingly carved by some long dead carpenter now ashen and charred black. Under the orange haze of the incandescent streetlight I could not hold back the tears.

I learned later that the church had been demolished for insurance reasons. No one wanted to pay the premiums on a structure now so rarely used.

I photographed what I couldn't help but feel was a crime scene. I knew when I reviewed my film the tears would likely return.

I took the drive home slowly, watching for racoons, moose, or anything else that might wander into my path. Driving down the lonely 620, back towards Freddy, the newly risen moon guided my path. It was like blue ribbon flowing across the landscape, almost hypnotizing in its gentle undulations over the hills. Struck by the celestially reflected sun, the barns and homesteads dotting my path shimmered like the ghosts of their long-passed builders. The spirits of the land rose from the soil, the histories of their lives coming together as one.

Despite the abuse of their legacies, perhaps some relic of meaning would remain. Their stories await to be found, and someday mine too, in the grand mulch of history.

In the days following I selected my photos and printed them. I barely shed a tear as it turns out, though I felt one welling up as I looked on the dying church. I submitted my assignment timely, though the portfolio turned out substantially bigger than originally expected.

"A very sombre work," said my professor, looking briefly at the graded print-out.

"I thought so too, but did you get any feeling of a subtle warmth anywhere at all?"

"I suppose so, but I'd have to look closely again to be sure."

## In the Wind
### *for M.K.S.*


If you walk the same path every day through the woods
clearing the way in your coming and going

you know when branches have fallen. Each branch downed
has a trace of the wind of descent vibrating through it.

In the time between coming and going,
in the rain of branches from the understory,

you can read the night, the wind, the lack of it,
what has happened back to happening.

The forest is sloughing dead to make room for the sun.
And you, bent there to gather branches,

have always been walking
the dark woods children hurry through

to get where they are going—
yet the forest is the coming and the going.

—Lee Sharkey

## Wood Lot in April

I lose the trail, or it eludes
me. Led astray, the bent-down saplings
keep their flex, may even rise.

Death rises from the older dead in branches.
The blown-down spruce, still green, begin
their shriveling. Their bride-white snow

has fled. *Look alive*, some cheery
voice might say. The spruce comply, for now,
unlike the ash leaves, last year's fall,

colored sawdust and cinder, papering
the sucking mud. We're all ground up,
huddled under another blow-down

where the wind marshalled its strength,
and then let go without a target.

—Michele Leavitt

# One Letter Away: A Word Ladder

Trees were a prime factor in the development of Maine's Penobscot River watershed. Over the centuries, human hunger and greed have turned raw timber into refined lumber, supply to demand, want into need. Among the first of these transformers were European prospectors who came to the Maine woods in the seventeenth century, displacing the native Wabanaki inhabitants in search of white pines, hundreds of feet tall and hundreds of years old:

PINE is what the King needed for his navy ships, so he called them
MINE, and marked them with his axes. His men proceeded to
MINT riches from the wilderness, sent each pine floating through the
MIST above the river, each destined to become a
MAST.

European settlers begged, borrowed, and stole land from the Wabanaki as they pushed farther north, into the pines, cutting and building as they went. By the time of the American Revolution, sawmills crowded the lower river banks.

TREE
FREE from the roots, and the eagle did
FLEE her nest in the high pine branches, she
FLEW high as eyes could see. Below the loggers
SLEW them down like giants, like a
SLAW a mix of tangled sticks, then—
LAWS at their backs, time on their side—men with
SAWS cut the jackstraws into smaller bits,
SAGS beneath their tired eyes, jams in the current forced
LAGS in delivery, eventually they sent them floating to the sea, billions of
LOGS.

Waterways carried the cut timber from the forest to the mills. Logging companies reshaped brooks, dynamited streams into chutes, flattened falls, widened narrows, blasted boulders, and straightened tight curves to drive the logs downstream. Walls of rock and timber funnelled the current to spinning wheels.

FOREST as far as the eye can see, birch, maple, ash, oak, and
SOFTER grain of spruce, fir, and pine; the logger becomes a
SIFTER of the straight, tall and true, a
SILTER of streams where
SILVER salmon spawn.
SOLVER of downstream demand, he
SOLVES the jam with dynamite and dams, no
SALVES for these wounds, dripping sap. He
SLAVES away through winter, trunks skidding over frozen
SLADES with no way down come spring but through the spinning
BLADES of sawmills. The lumber baron
BLAMES seething soils, teeming current slowing down the log drive,
BLAMER of rocks and shallows, curves that
RAMBLE in the wabe
RUMBLE, rumble, boil and bubble, the forest flows downstream to be
LUMBER.

In the middle of the nineteenth century, as the lumber trade was reaching its peak, technological advances made it possible to make paper from wood pulp instead of cloth rags. Logging, dam-building, and flooding expanded.

WOODS were here for millennia, but demand grew for
WORDS, and the Penobscot Indians, once guardians of the place now
WARDS of the state, take their spears, baskets, and other
WARES, escape the rising water to watch from the islands as each stranger
PARES away his land, each
PARER in service to the mills, who crush the trees into
PAPER.

It wasn't long before technology made it possible to make electricity from falling water. Mill owners, towns, and entrepreneurs built new dams and converted old dams to generate energy. Throughout the Penobscot River watershed, the dams went up: ten, twenty, one hundred, and more.

FALLS, where water rushes like Alice down a rabbit hole, the rapid
PALLS as up go walls of rock and timber, the river's fury
PALES, from moving water to still water,
POLES apart. Fish cannot swim, men cannot eat, a
POLER cannot move a boat through current captured for electrical
POWER.

For hundreds of years the dams stayed put, until June 2012, when the Penobscot Indian Nation and other members of the Penobscot River Restoration Trust breached the Great Works Dam at Old Town, allowing the river to flow freely through the rapids for the first time in nearly 200 years.


DAMS block the flow of water, and the future
DIMS for all of us, no
DIME or nickel can save this system, in
DIRE shape at the end of the twentieth century. Then, under the
WIRE, a compromise! A plan! to end the days of paper roses and electric
WINE, to force the grip of industry to
WANE, to restore and remake a river
ANEW.

—Catherine Schmitt

# Lost and Found Logs

Charles McGowan

During the heyday of the timber industry in Maine not all logs made it through the drives to sorting booms and sawmills. Some hung up and rotted on shore, a few that could not float on their own were part of rafts that broke up in sluices, gorges, rapids, and storms. Others laid in river pools or lake water and sank.

Maine and New Brunswick log recovery companies sustained a unique version of the lumber industry by salvaging those logs. Sunken pulpwood was raised from the bottom of the Madawaska River by New Brunswick's Fraser Company from 1955 to the early '70s because it was becoming a pollution hazard. In winter, they would cut holes in the ice, use pike poles to find and "fish" the four-footers out, and slide them out onto the ice with a pulp hook. When there was no safe ice, they worked from rafts. Much of that salvaged wood was reusable and went to the paper mill in Edmunston, New Brunswick.

During a 1920s winter, a logger named Louis Woodbury "Woody" Eaton did it out of immediate necessity on a drive through a log-holding bay in the St. Croix River. Born in Calais, Maine, in 1892, Eaton grew up working in the timberlands. He advanced to top level management in family-owned Eaton Land Company that had holdings in Maine and New Brunswick. In 1954, he wrote Pork, Molasses and Timber, Stories of Bygone Days in the Logging Camps of Maine. Woody probably had a license to hunt and fish, but his trademark was a literary license to play with place names by spelling them backwards. "Notae River," probably the St. Croix, was derived from Eaton. "Hamot" was Tomah Mountain and Stream in Washington County, Maine. I wonder if he was carried backwards from Calais when he was buried across the border with his parents in the St. Stephen, New Brunswick Rural Cemetery?

Woody pioneered in the lost-andfound log business. Hardwood sank unless rafted when floated. Rough driving conditions caused breakups and logs were lost. Logs held back from the drive by low water sometimes sank. Woody's challenge was delivering enough logs to the mills when they ran out. Though underwater then for only a few seasons, he raised and recovered enough lost logs to keep the mills busy and food on the tables of the men who worked there.

With a 5–15% loss of river driven logs, the lumbering industry took "sinkage" for granted. Through modern search and retrieval methods, preserved logs that were under water for over 80 years have been raised for lumber. The tight grain and aged finish, when sawn and milled, produces prized furniture and stock for musical instruments. Cross-border companies have reclaimed Bird's-Eye Maple, Yellow Birch, Red Oak, White Pine, Spruce, Eastern Hemlock, and lesser-known species such as Butternut and Basswood.

Shaw & Tenney paddle and oar makers of Orono crafted a limited edition of L.L.Bean centennial paddles in 2012. The Bean paddle wood was retrieved from the depths of Quakish Lake on the Penobscot River by West Branch Heritage Timber of Millinocket. I was drawn to a lightweight beavertail paddle with a unique grain. Some paddles were clear and handsome from the grip to the tip, but I picked this one because of its likeness to a bateau or canoe set pole with the blade having a semblance to flowing streams or rock-ridden rapids.

Edited from *CROSS BORDER TALES, MAINE, NEW BRUNSWICK, AND *MORE**, 2015, by Charles E. McGowan

# What It Is For

Cheryl Savageau

But what is it for? She asks me as we drive through the forest of tiny trees. They are no more than four feet tall, these high desert trees. They are not babies, they are full grown, like the scrub pines on Cape Cod. I am lost in this nation of trees, on this road somewhere near Taos, New Mexico. I am used to the Maples of the northeast, I walk in their shade. So this is what they call a forest here. I know that's not really true, I've seen the tall Pines that grow up at Los Alamos, on the mountain road I drive from Albuquerque to Santa Fe, the road I prefer because they are there. But it pleases me to be amongst this forest of tiny trees, their difference charms me. Any time I travel, I'm afraid I'll get there and it will be unfamiliar, alien, but when I step off the plane, I realize, oh, yes, this is the earth, and take a trusting breath.

She is talking again, and I switch my attention from the Land outside the car to her words. But *what is it for,* she asks again. I don't understand the question. I think maybe I'm not paying close enough attention, distracted as I am by the trees. But it is the trees she is talking about. You know, she says, gesturing with her left hand as she steers with her right. All this. All this, she says, *what is it for?*

What do you mean what is it for?

You know, is it for farming, or dairy, or ranching...you know, what is it for?

*What is it for*? It's for itself, I say. She shakes her head in frustration.

This conversation has become emblematic—those moments of cultural dissonance in so many conversations, when I realize the underpinnings of our conversations are different, that what I think we are talking about is not it at all.

When I was in my twenties, my then husband's aunt was concerned at what she considered my "atheism." I never said I was an atheist. It's not a word I would use, based on a negative, a lack of something, rather than on a positive presence that I felt but could't express. How can you not believe in God? she asked. How do you know what is good or evil? What will you teach your children?

I remember the question being so much bigger than I, at that time in my life, could answer in this short conversation over the kitchen table. I did't know how to talk about the sacred. I felt instead an abyss, an absence of words, one that led me to become a poet. I could only tell her that I could't believe in that personal God, that old man in the sky. There were so many assumptions that we did't share. I didn't yet know our Abenaki word, Ktsiniwes—Great Mystery—that sacred mysterious matrix of infinite becoming.

*What is it for?* The language that inhabits her, that inhibits her, says that these trees, this forest are objects. What I see as beings, as a nation of trees, she sees as, not exactly non-living, because she would admit that trees are alive, in a limited way, but they have no sovereignty, no personhood. They exist only in relation to human needs. Which means they are expendable. This place should be "for" something that humans need. Otherwise, what?

I could have said that they were "for" making oxygen, that they might hold some medicine that we don't even know about, that they hold together the soil in this arid place and provide food, make a home for a vast population of birds, insects, reptiles, mammals, invertebrates. But that is not what they are "for." These are gifts they give freely. Our proper response is gratitude.

What is it for? She turned on the radio. I looked out the window. The Land extended in all its beauty, in all its mystery. This Forest, this Nation.

## Le Barachois

*Fort Daniel Quebec, June 2013*

Sous ma fenétre,
sur le barachois placide,
les mouettes, et les canards
quarelle—jusqu'en un aigle glisser au-dessus.

Une giboulée,
le soleil retourne.

Le monde et le vent
embrassent le tranquilité

L'aigle voler dans
les bras des montagnes.

Tous les oiseaux chanter encore.

—Bruce Pratt

## The Barachois

*Fort Daniel Quebec, June 2013*

Beneath my window
on the placid barachois,
gulls and ducks quarrel
until an eagle glides above.

A sudden shower,
the sun returns.

The world and wind
embrace the stillness.

The eagle flies into
the arms of the mountains.

The birds sing again.

—Bruce Pratt

## On the Way

An afternoon breeze. The tidal water retreats—mudflats gleam and pucker, boulders hunker against a tumbled cloud-sky. And now the gulls come, claim the rocks with their unmelodious shrieks. Single-minded, they wait. Her own days are ambitious, her dreams troubled. And her chores—hanging laundry, splitting wood—don't ever feel conclusive.

In the rain, the garden closes in on itself. Paths turn slippery, foliage deepens. Without a god to assign them, blessings move freely—an elusive flutter, a borderless place. She swims into the bay's cold expanse. Her daughter arrives, carries her luggage up the wooden stairs, the home's musical scales. A blessing may feel smooth like the stone-grey water.

Today, broken clouds skim the earth, granting a partial view at what lies beyond. Her daughter's body bulges lightly over the belly-baby. For mammals it's normal, of course, but still a shock, this first showing. Rain has swelled the streams. A waterfall—in the heat, they clamber on mossy boulders and dowse themselves. *Attendere*—to stretch like dancers, to attend toward light-filled canopies.

Last night there was music—live in the rain, a wooden stage, raised among the trees' dripping green. A bonfire illumined dancers, their hands rising like sparks, their feet molding wet clay. Among microphones, monitors, pitch and motion, sometimes the players' faces would lose themselves, the drums keep the beat on their own.

When she stores the garden tools, last sunlight seeps into the forest. She takes a moment to smooth her forehead, realign joints—blessings need sustenance. Her daughter will soon be parting, leaving behind a more vibrant house—watercolor tints, night vision's larger range. Is she afraid of the obvious? The self-disperses after death. Walking, she feels for moss, for roots under foot—the obvious, from *ob viam*: on the way.

—Leonore Hildebrandt

# Agronomist, Meteorologist, Mechanic, Midwife

In the manure spattered,
plank-sided box stall,
bellows of travail swell,
pursuing us like a horsefly
out for blood
as we go on
carrying buckets of fresh milk,
warm as a baby's bath water,
to the cooler,
throwing hay down from the mow,
breaking open the bales,
doling out the dusty flakes,
spreading clean shavings,
smacking with the scent of pine
beneath barrel shaped bodies.

Behind the wooden screen,
worn smooth by flanks of filing cattle,
the first-calf heifer, winnowed by pain,
weakens in hope.
Dad slides the iron bolt,
steps inside wearing rubber boots,
his shirt sleeves rolled up,
carrying a coil of rope.
Only the top of his head,
the faded denim hat
could be seen at work
striving against the odds.

A sudden settling down the line,
an assembled sigh,
primordial moans dissolve

into tender murmurs
for the newborn,
glistening like a slick stone
in a stream.
When Dad steps out
there is relief in his eyes,
satisfaction on his shoulders—
he has tipped the balance of nature.

—Joyce Lorenson

## Heirloom

The problem is that I was looking
for a tomato I'd already eaten.
It was two years ago at a summer
writing retreat and writing had exhausted me
and I'd gone out for green beans.

At the farm stand the farmer
told me there were green and yellow beans
but none picked, and I offered to help.
Turns out the heat doesn't stop
even when you're picking someone else's beans.

I asked her what kinds she grew. She told me
they were from plants her uncle had grown
and saved seeds from over many years,
so long ago that the name was lost
and they just called them Uncle Harry's beans,

or Uncle Harvey or Lewis, I have to admit
that it's been long enough I can't recall.
She told me he'd been dead a dozen years,
but his wife, her aunt, had died just that morning
at age 102. Not a surprise except

she'd been independent right up until the end,
not without her problems but independent.
And all I could say was *Oh*.
I thought of her uncle and aunt and picked beans
and sweated and bought the whole box of them,

even though it was so much more than I needed.
As an afterthought, I picked up that tomato

and bought it, too. Medium size, an heirloom
like Brandywine, maybe, perfectly ripe.
Later, making my meal alone in a house occupied

by other writers and one painter on their own retreats,
I cooked the green beans and sliced the tomato.
The green beans were very good,
Uncle Harry's or Harvey's beans, as expected,
no better or worse than the ones I grew.

The tomato was the surprise—still so early
in the season but hearty, rich, perfect. I shut my eyes.
I thought of Neruda's "Ode to the Tomato." I thought
of the word heirloom, of the taste of good things
passed down to us, in old recipes and ways

of growing and farmers watching
which plants produced the best fruit.
Two years would go by, me looking
for that tomato again, everywhere,
and not really finding it. Thinking sometimes

of Uncle Harry's or Harvey's beans,
and annoyed at myself about the tomato,
because I hadn't asked her about it at all.
Two years later, and me not knowing
if anyone had saved the seeds.

—Karen Skolfield

## A Price to Pay

My parents didn't know
How to be
Grandparents
Of faraway children

*Mis hijos* didn't know
How to be
Grandchildren
Of distant adults

Like a permanent marker on a white board
My migration leaves a visible shadow
Rarely muffled
Often murmuring

Of things lost

—Emma Suárez-Báez

# Names Properly

My mother's maiden name rolls on the breath,
tongue soft against the teeth, the final *n*
all but lost—*Drouin.*

Her married name's tougher at the start,
tongue tip tight against the teeth: *Te, te*
like the tut of a flag

in stiff weather, like the clip of my *pepère's*
ax in the north woods. The *h, l* and final *t*
all bear my father's silent

weight, his *sais pas,* his melodic humming.
The *r* growls from the back of the throat,
glottal. Controlled.

I practice speaking both names properly—
*Drouin et Theriault,* the only French
I was given.

I learned the English names of things: *tenement*
and *church. Split shift* and *overtime.* No *maison.*
No *eglise. Ma mère* smothered

in the sea of otherness. *Mon père* sounding
like something swollen and still. I retrieved
my lost language

from textbooks, learned it as a visitor to my life.
*Drouin et Theriault* – an early song, I've kept
all along – wind in trees, thread

unwinding from factory spools.
The feathery quilts *qui mes grands-mères*
*ont toujours fait.*

—Jeri Theriault

# How a Community of Women

*Resolved, That we will not go back into the mills to work unless our*
*wages are continued...as they have been.*

*Resolved, That none of us will go back, unless they receive us all as one.*

*Resolved, That if any have not money enough to carry them home, they*
*shall be     supplied.*

—*Boston Evening Transcript*, February 18, 1834


How my French Canadian great grandmother and great-great
        aunts toiled thirteen hours a day in the textile mills of
        Lowell, Massachusetts.
How weak the light when they left the boardinghouse each morning.
How screaming starlings flash mobbed them along the way.
How they sucked thread through the eye of their foot-long wooden
        shuttles that fed the cotton to the looms.
How they called that quick motion of their lips "the kiss of death."
How they could not converse over the cacophonic, clickity-click,
        clickity-clack of five hundred howling looms.
How they walked back in ear-ringing darkness, had dinner, then
        took up their needlework—crochet, crewel, cross stitch,
        knitting, mending, quilting, darning—close work, women's
        work.
My mother taught me, her mother taught her, her mother taught her.

—Cindy Veach

# Homecoming

Irish on my mother's side.
My grandmother jeered
at the *diddly diddly* music
and turned on Perry Como.
We grandchildren drank
too much and cursed the English
in Irish pubs on the Cape
because the songs told us to.

French on my dad's side.
Teachers with phony accents
scoffed at our half-hearted attempts.
We watched French Canadians
in tiny bathing suits
roam our beach eating raw shellfish
from the shoreline, and too many men
on the ice at the Montreal Forum.

Decades later, we cross the Bay of Fundy,
heading for Digby
for the land of Acadians and two boat Irish.
First sight draws such a longing,
a held breath awakening,
an aching heart homecoming,
the double leaving,
the harbored hard history.

—David R. Surette

# The Abyssal Plains

I

Sometimes when we go down by the old Narragansett casino
I can still see glimmers of my haunted youth all those empty
summer fields full of fireflies; fireworks and 4th of July sparklers
in everybody else's driveway, sometimes making it look like
Luna Park on the cover of *The Great Gatsby*, husbands and wives
fighting like only they have a past:

Nothing *"...makes you love me! makes you want to help me!"*

Lost behind their taillights are the old ways, the peaceful air of youth,
wet, shimmering emerald in our hands: a timeless artifact only kept
alive by oral tradition, all those other half dispositions and relics
laying on card tables or in the chest of draws in Chippendales no one
ever wants to open up again.

II

When I am back in the warmth of beautiful New England it fills my
sails with wind, I am back in her, dark in the Sohms, in embryonic
fluid, in the abyssal plains, her heartbeat close again, the ghosts
of Pequots and Narragansetts behind every river birch or squalor
rock;

I can remember summers on Rhode Island salt ponds: Moonstone
and Jerusalem and Roy Carpenter's Beach back when they only had
Algonquian names, all that black bear meat we used to roast on open
spits down along the shores of Ninigret Pond, the local waters so
verdant and azure all us native people believe this was where God
dipped his paint brush after painting the sky blue;

yet when I return one summer to my ancient and sacred lands I am
first met by the façade of a shopping mall, a real glimpse of death,
a first bitter taste of oleander and darkness, a weight and hopelessness
that could only have been put into place by the most mindless  wrecking
crew of all time (mankind)—

a sallow reflection of light wavers down under the Newport Bridge on
waters we once used to race home on to a place that is better left like it
never existed (for expedience and progress' sake, they say).

*Mat coanaumwaúmis!*

—Jéanpaul Ferro

# Over the Wall

Dan Crowfeather McIsaac

There was a time, more years ago than I care to count, when I was going through Basic Training after joining the Armed Forces. As part of our training, we had to run the "Confidence" course— military speak for an obstacle course. Typical of such courses, ours had a very high wooden wall, which was deliberately made much too high for any but the strongest and most agile jumpers to climb alone. Like so many other things in Basic Training, the purpose of this obstacle was to teach us about teamwork. Here's how it worked: the first two to reach the wall boosted the third person until they could reach the top. The third person then stayed at the top of the wall, reaching down to grab the hand of the next person as they were boosted up, and helping them climb to the top. As the helpers tired, they were relieved by others, who would continue to help until everyone had succeeded in climbing over this wall. Some had an easier time than others, but nobody was left behind. This activity, and others like it, were what built the unique sense of brotherhood that all of us who served are privileged to share. We learned to depend on our brothers-in-arms, and they learned to depend on us.

Many years ago, it was the same in First Nation cultures. Every person would readily help their brother or sister, and enjoyed the security of knowing that they could count on that help being returned if they needed it. Every person felt that sense of brotherhood or sisterhood with the others in their village or clan. Everyone understood, without having to try, that you yourself get ahead when you help your neighbour get ahead. Finally, when the first Europeans arrived on these shores, that same helping hand was extended to them, because to do any less was simply unthinkable. Unfortunately for the Red Man, most Europeans came from cultures that focused on the individual rather than the group, and dog-eat-dog became the new world order.

Time has passed, and history has seen terrible things done to the first peoples of this land. And those things have taken a terrible toll, because they have destroyed our proud tradition of working together as a team. History seems to have taught us that if someone else begins to succeed, we somehow lose something in their success. When someone begins to rise above the years of oppression and pain, and begins to reach for a way out of the trap, the people around take notice. However, rather than helping, it seems that all too often petty jealousies surface, and the whispering starts, and in most cases the person is dragged back just as they have put their hand to the top of the wall. This has happened for so long that most no longer even try, preferring to live their lives in pain and hopelessness rather than take the risk of being outcasts in their own societies. In the end, only the strongest and most agile manage to free themselves from the walls that have been built around our people.

I believe it is time for a return to one of the oldest and most powerful values of the old cultures. It is time for us to realize that we can help the person next to us without lessening ourselves. We need to remember that by helping others to rise, we help ourselves to rise as well. As I learned so long ago in Boot Camp, only teamwork will help us to overcome the biggest obstacles that surround us. We can no longer wait for help from the Government, or indeed from anyone else — we must all look within, and learn what strengths we have to share, and help ourselves to do what must be done. If we see someone who is trying to make something of themselves despite the barriers imposed by the outside world, we need to support them in any way we can, and depend on them to reach back and help us when they are able.

I am no blind optimist. I know that sometimes the ones who reach the top of the wall will simply vault over and be gone, with no thought for those left behind. However, I also know that, if enough people choose to believe in each other, and choose to continue that belief even when they are disappointed, the years of harm can be undone and we can once again stand strong together. We can create a new way of thinking, a new concept of what is normal behaviour. We can set a good example for our youth, and teach them to work towards an end to the pain and hopelessness. This end will not come through Government money or from outside agencies; this end will come from the strength of character that is ours by birthright, but which we seem to have misplaced somewhere among the gambling tables and empty bottles.

My brothers and sisters, the walls are everywhere, and they are very high indeed. But they are not too high if we work together. Come—give me your hand....

*Taho! Msit No'kmaq*

# Downeast Odyssey: a trilogy of ultra-short stories

Chuck Kniffen

## Tommy Quits Mayberry

Thirteen. Kicked by a cow, clawed by a cat, attacked by a monkey, rat bit, skunk bit, Tommy bites the bully. All before to the tumble over the waterfall.

Three years pass, he impresses friends with fifteen belly flops from Big Dock, totals Pop's panel wagon in an extravagant rollover, puts out lit cigarettes on his chest, chugs a jug of Southern Comfort while doing the Hop on Captain Fitch's favorite table, and totals Pop's Toyota trying to swallow Molly's tongue at 70 miles per hour on Long Cove Road.

His body neon flesh beneath an orange mop flashes a riot of color: bright red, dead white, puckered swamp green on bilge water black, purple and crimson stripes streaking across fields of oozing yellow and the ever present blue on beige of the bone hard stone lonely pecker.

"*Soldier Boy*," Tommy sings, packing his bag.

## 'Nam in a Nutshell

"NO!"
"Pussy."
"No."
"Wimp ass mother...."

Three days of jungle, rain, bullets, and bugs, Decareaux had been at Tommy to bust out his tooth with a broken bayonet. It was killing him. He was killing Tommy.

That night a half-ton bomb fell five miles from out of a B52. Shrapnel big as a dragon's jawbone cleaved the Creole wide open, spread entrails over forty yards of defoliated forest. What to do? Tommy stomps on his neck and blows his skull to King-fucking-dom come. He also shears off a fistful of his finest toes.

Useless now and back in the world, Mom whips up a batch of spaghetti and meatballs with his favorite sauce for supper. Later, Tommy visits his buddy's girl Kathy. She gives some swell head and asks, "Would you like another piece of chocolate cake?"

"YOU BET!"

### Not Only the Good

Cold coffee, bitter grounds burrow, black holes in brown teeth, fire's out, the dog a gaunt reminder. Hunkered in a flap-door shack, Tommy shivers, creeping dread and bleeding fear, no knights errant will slay the ogre demanding its due, pound for pound, flesh to ground, he watches darkness row slowly across expanding skies. Just another two fingers and couple of kickers would do.

Snap that shit. Such gravitas is morbid, crushes the bloom. Fat Betty fresh out of Wounded Sisters U. drops by, tired of box lunches at the Y. She got money, Fingerhut pie, and half a pack of Pall Malls. Taras Bulba rises, shear the shackles, leap the stile, they flee the dead strait. Is that blood on a tiger's tooth or a knife in the mouth of the machine? The promise looms, exquisite in detail. Laughing at the rage the fight is joined.

# Names

Crows could be named like British battleships—
        Formidable, Intrepid, Dreadnought—
Weighty appellations, or jaunty like destroyers—
        Excelsior, Artful, Sentinel—
Never Whimsy or Nonchalance, which
Crows keep to themselves

We may name eagles for great battles—
        Vera Cruz, Antietam, Midway—
Call sparrows for fighter planes—
        Spitfire, Lightning.
Gulls, idiosyncratic bombers, may be
        Lady Luck, Georgia Peach, Enola Gay.

But tell me, crows, if I am to know,
It must come from you: what name
Captures flashes of light off
Your terrible black,
        Explosive as your eyes.

—Michael R. Brown

## Waverly and the C-Notes

Waverly was sure that the man, Hansen, who lived—squatted—in the house at the end of the road, was stealing tools from him. Because the road ran between Waverly's house and his garage, there was no way to keep Hansen off the premises. It was a town road and Hansen had the right to pass over it.

Hansen's house was a field back from Waverly's. Back then it was no more than a field hut with two rooms and a porch made of scavenged lumber tacked on—rickety, sagging, every angle askew.

Waverly had caught Hansen in the garage more than once and each time Hansen threatened the old man. Such threats were to be taken seriously. It was known by the nighttime screams and the morning-after bruises that Hansen beat his wife and his son. Those two looked alike with their broad, flat faces and perpetually startled eyes. Hansen also had periodic brushes with the sheriff and was generally known to be a drunk, a thief, and a cheat.

Waverly was beside himself that such a "devil" had moved into the village. Up to that point, none of us had ever locked our doors, day or night. Sometime about then, my wife and I had the porch light fixed. We began to lock up at night. One August morning I saw Waverly standing in the lane, purple-faced, waving his arms. There had been yet another altercation in the garage. Waverly was an excitable man and sometimes comically so, tho' nobody would dare laugh. Besides, everybody was on his side in this matter.

He was in his mid-80s. There was the danger that one of his transports would carry him off.

When the "aaaaahh boys," the goddammits and sonofabitches finally eased off, Waverly lectured me about the moral degeneration that had overtaken Maine and ruined the whole country since the days of his childhood. Once upon a time, he said, his grandfather had laid $100 bills, weighted down by stones, along the whole length of the lane from the paved road to his house. This was to prove a point: anybody could easily have taken them, but nobody would or did.

The putative bills sat out there for a day and a night. I almost believed the story on account of the sheer beauty of the image. I saw that whole quarter mile of dirt lane flickering with C-notes.

*crisp notes*
*the flash of birch leaves*
*in the wind*

—Frederick Lowe

# Spring Pick-up

Dozens of mattresses line the road,
neighbors tossing beds as if
the hotel bed bug blight
had reached down east.

Some are stacked like the princess
and the pea while others float
like rafts on brown shoulders, taking in
the rain and, yes, it's Maine,

a coating of snow, which
makes you shiver, whose dreams
shift to Arctic places whenever
your wife pulls the comforter away

in her troubled sleep.
Miserable things, not the body count
your mother called streetside bags
of garbage in the city, more morose

than that, unfit for making love,
for even meanest slumber unless you're
homeless and exploring Somesville
in April, in which case

you can't believe your luck, a bed
every hundred yards or so
buttressing the cold road
awaiting the blissful collapse

of your worn and wandering body.

—Carl Little

## Taking Off the Plates

For three months we kept the plates on, reminding us how
far we had come. "California" repeating itself inside the
ears, over and over like a mantra.

Painting the old saltbox and resurrecting the shaggy
lilac out front
because we could not understand how else to start but on
        the outside.
It was the International Bridge over the Narrows that finally
brought us to our senses:

the heart's actions
are neither the coming nor the going.

And so we came to apply the jewelweed growing wild
by the roadside
to the rash of poison ivy.
Drove the car to Calais and exchanged plates.

—Kathleen Ellis

# Wapizagonke

I

All night I was gliding
down a long narrow Canadian lake
in the wake of summer—

on the cusp of autumn—
with the wind-song of a native woman
echoing off the cliffs.

All night I was drifting
in and out toward dawn, fearing to fall asleep
in the arms of winter.

II

All morning I've been waiting
for her to float through my kitchen window
carrying the paddles,

scuffing her deerskin boots
on the boards. Waiting for her to startle
me awake with her tears.

All morning I've been dreaming
of her out on the water under the stars
singing me her song.

—John Perrault

# Allegiance

I tried to lie on the crumbly
red granite of Passamaquoddy Bay
to listen, to join the great flowing
currents, rip tides, whirlpools,
to embrace the St. Croix,
Cobscook, reversing falls
lean into the curves thru Sipayik,
longed to paddle the grand lakes,
around Motahkomikuk, Spedneck,
undo the arbitrary lines
between homelands.

But the pink granite of Penobscot Bay,
the resonant slow thunk
pulled me back to the high rounded nubs
leapfrogging across it, Schoodic
Cadillac, Megunticook, my hips
molding more easily around the
archipelago protecting the Passagasawakeag,
Naskaeg and Brooklin, my blade
recognizing the Upper West Branch rills,
Chesuncook, and the long flow
out to Isle au Haut.

—Karin Spitfire

# Sweetfern

## Barbara Chatterton

The first man I kissed was a killer. He was 18; I had just turned 12. It was my second summer living in Machias, and my first year of raking blueberries. On the first day of the season, my mother dropped me off at the weighing station before the sun rose. There were already people waiting in small groups under the industrial lights that shone from the station's overhanging roof, and others soon arrived. I had no idea of what I was getting into—I was from out of state, my only previous experiences gathering blueberries were picnic outings with my grandmother. Everyone else on the crew came from families where raking was a rite of passage, or a necessity. My parents had decided I should spend the summer raking berries when I mentioned that the father of a girl from Sunday school owned a blueberry business. The experience, they said, would be good for me.

I bounced slightly on the balls of my feet at the edge of the milling group, hoping to be recognized, claimed, by someone in the small crowd. When the crew boss shouted, I followed everyone into the back of a truck and claimed a space on the wooden planks screwed down the length of the cargo area. Water and sack lunches were clenched between feet or knees and everyone had a blueberry rake. Mine was steel, about nine inches long, or thirty tine, and heavy before I'd even begun work. I looked, disbelieving, at the duct-taped, weld-warped, bent rakes the other rakers carried. They had to be at least twice as long as mine, and twice as heavy. Everyone's face looked doughy in the early morning gloom. Few people spoke, or even made eye contact. The adults seemed surly while the kids were simply dumb with weariness. As we rumbled into the dark mists that first morning, I was excited by the adventure and novelty of it.

I was deafened by the echoing roar of the engine as the truck banged and bumped toward our destination. Unable to hear what anyone was saying, increasingly nauseous from the diesel fumes, I passed the time studying the faces of the people around me. Toward the cab there was a group of girls I recognized from Sunday school who were studiously ignoring me. Opposite them sat a few boys, also from Sunday school, coolly looking beyond what was right in front of them, as if they weren't sitting on hard narrow benches and breathing exhaust fumes like the rest of us. A tall girl with high cheekbones and exotic eyes sitting alone seemed close to my age, but something about the random way her gaze flitted and then bore down on whatever was in her field of vision made me shrink against the hard metal wall of the truck, hoping she hadn't noticed me. The few adult women on the crew looked hard, angry. The men, easily making up half the crew, had massive necks and shoulders, their burled arms ending in hands as large as my face. They were perpetually hunched forward, postures coiled by resignation rather than eagerness. I later learned that they were clamdiggers, their bodies forever changed by years of heavy labor on the mudflats, but in those early days their unwieldy mass frightened me. Two men, sitting together across from me, were more normally sized. One looked out the open back of the truck at everything we were leaving behind— the town, the familiar roads, and eventually even unfamiliar paved roads were lost as we scraped down dirt tracks. The fog made it seem like everything was being erased behind us, and his expression revealed a sense of loss. His friend was more lighthearted and made faces at me until I shyly smiled back, awkward in the bright light of his cheery good looks.

*Children as young as twelve are allowed to rake, even today, but in the early 80's, children did not have to be accompanied by a guardian on the blueberry fields. In those days, there might be only one supervisory adult—the crew boss—on the field. The crew boss was responsible for driving the truck, moving the winnowing station, tallying the boxes in the field, and handling any issues that came up. Issues ranged from disagreements about who brought in how many buckets to fistfights to heatstroke. Children raked alongside adults, and if you didn't clear your rick fast enough, you were left behind in one section of the field while everyone else followed the winnowing station as it arced from the beginning of the field slowly toward the end, its progress marked by towering stacks of boxed berries. At the end of the day, these pillars of wooden crates were loaded onto a truck by a field crew who brought everything back to the weighing station and compared the actual boxes to the field tally sheets.*

*When you rake blueberries, there are things you quickly learn to make your life on the field more bearable. You learn to freeze water in big soda bottles the night before, grabbing them from the freezer on your way out in the morning. Through the early hours of the day you thank God for the cool, refreshing water as the ice melts. Later, the water becomes warm and stale and tastes of plastic but you drink it anyway to avoid heatstroke. If you are girl, you learn how to pee quickly and discreetly in the wild, to avoid tell-tale splashes on socks or sneakers.*

The truck lurched to a stop and everyone jumped off to gather loosely. I copied what I saw the others do, leaving my lunch but bringing my rake and water. Once everyone was on the ground, Mr. Burns, the crew chief, began shouting orders in a hoarse voice. I was distracted from what he was saying by the strange landscape. No two spots of ground were the same—one spot was a thin, sandy skim of pale soil while next to that was a shock of dark green leaves comically overburdened with small, purplish berries and beside that was a thrust of gray-white rock pointing accusingly at the sky. Everywhere were white threads that turned the field into orderly strips six feet wide but with irregular lengths. The straight strings were like a mirage against the wild, unruly landscape. I couldn't tell if they ever ended, or if my eyes simply failed to pick them out in the shrouded distance. The mist itself managed to be both dark and light at once as the sun, an indistinct silver coin overhead, began its job of burning off the moisture. I shivered as the cool droplets gathered on my T-shirt and the fringe of my cutoff jeans. Mr. Burns gestured toward me and the other kids in a way that looked like he was gathering us up. We shuffled toward him and he immediately excused the boys with a short speech.

"You fellas have all either been here before or know someone who has. Rake clean, and stay out of the way of the adults. Start with a rick near the truck and the faster you finish, the better you get to pick for next time. But I'll warn you, rake dirty and you'll be stuck on cleanup for the rest of the day. Got it?" The boys nodded, pulling bent baseball caps out of back pockets and positioning them low on their foreheads. Their grim expressions struck me as comically over-acted while sending tendrils of worry through my belly. What if this was not going to be as fun as I'd thought?

Mr. Burns turned toward the remaining girls and looked at us solemnly. He was tall with a belly that hung over his jeans. His leathery skin was burned red, making him look perpetually angry despite his doleful expression.

"I don't care for having young girls out on the field with grown men," he began, "but this is what we've got." He sighed and looked out toward the forest that ringed the blueberry field. "I don't want anyone going out alone for rest-breaks. You girls need to stick together, if you understand what I mean." He looked at us. "It might be difficult for some of the men to remember you're just girls." His eyes rested briefly on the tall girl with the jittery gaze, then swept round to me. "Anyway, safety first. Agreed?"

The Sunday school girls nodded knowingly, but I was confused. I wanted to ask him what he meant, but I worried that the other girls would tease me if I did. I swallowed and nodded, Mr. Burns' eyes dark on mine.

"Okay," he clapped, the sound jarringly loud in the quiet air. "I want you girls here, closest to the truck. Pick a rick, rake it clean, and move to the next empty one. We're heading thataway," he gestured loosely in the direction some of the largest men had headed toward.

"The raking's better down there, but we have to clean out this section first. Keep moving, get it done. You heard me tell the boys that if I catch you being sloppy, you'll be put on cleanup detail as punishment." He stopped and looked measuringly at each of us. "Get to work."

The other girls quickly claimed their rows, leaving the tall girl and I standing aimlessly by the truck. I shuffled over to the first empty strip and looked down the length of it. The other girl came up behind me and stood silently until I noticed her.

"You need buckets." She pointed toward the truck. I noticed a pile of white buckets with metal handles. When she took two, I did the same.

"Easier to stay balanced with two," she explained. Mystified, I nodded.

She took the rick beside mine, turning one of her buckets upside down to make a chair. I stood at the opening edge of my row and hefted my rake, surreptitiously trying to see what everyone else was doing with theirs. I saw the girls nearby bend over and pull their rakes through the plants on the ground, then dump the berries into their buckets. It looked simple enough.

Directly before me was a lush expanse of berries and I jabbed my rake into it, driving the long tines into the meager soil. I yanked the rake out, noticing that I'd smashed a number of berries and knocked others off their plants. They rolled under leaves and I fumbled to pick them up with my fingers. For my next swipe with the rake, I went too high and knocked more berries loose, and lost more time picking them up with my fingers, Mr. Burns' warning about cleanup crew duty burning in the back of my mind.

Finally, I managed to get through the brief section of thick berries and found myself in a miniature jungle. The blueberries were there, but so were tiny trees with smooth gray-brown trunks and glossy leaves with nibbled-looking edges. There were bushy plants that looked like ferns with jagged-but-soft dark leaves, and there were tall, spindly ferns with graceful fronds hanging down. And there were rocks—small rocks that ambushed my rake and caused my berries to spill across the crumbly ground, big rocks that attracted the most heavily-laden plants but made it impossible for me to collect the fat berries with my rake, and wide expanses of flat, flecked rock where nothing grew. As I worked my way along, I noticed a powerful smell, sweetly intoxicating. I thought it was the smell of the blueberry barren, of the land itself. It was stronger where I stood now, but I realized I had been smelling it all morning.

Far ahead of me were the Sunday school girls; behind me, the quiet girl with the wild eyes had finally gotten off her bucket and was methodically sweeping her arm back and forth, back and forth, across the width of her rick. She would catch up to me soon, despite the fact that she had started so much later. The mist had burned off and the air felt fresh and warm. I bent back into my labor. I tried to mimic her long, sweeping motions, but almost every time I hit something that caused my berries to spill out of the rake and scatter across the ground. I looked at the ground I'd already cleared and saw telltale spots of blue, proof that I was slow and dirty. A dirty raker. The shame settled over my stooped back, an extra layer of gravity.

*To rake blueberries effectively, you lean into the sweeping motion, bending slightly at the knees and using your legs as well as your shoulders to carry your rake through the sweep. This adds more power to your motion, better supports your back, and reduces the fatigue on your shoulders. Novice rakers who are unaware of proper form often bend at the waist and use their shoulder muscles to power through the motions. By the end of the day, the back pain from a poor posture can be intense. Keep your rake slightly upturned, ensuring the berries roll down into the reservoir area behind the long tines, and empty the contents of the rake regularly rather than trying to overfill it. Not only does this limit losses should the rake get hung up on something, but it also prevents the berries from being crushed. Each filled bucket roughly translates to one box of winnowed berries, or $2.50.*

*You carry your filled buckets to the nearest winnowing station, which is set far ahead of where the crew starts raking to cut down on how many times the winnower has to be hauled onto a truck and driven further down-field, and then wait in line to carefully dump your berries onto the conveyer mechanism that will blow leaves, sticks, and debris away from the berries that collect in the wooden crate underneath. You learn there are tricks to winnowing, tricks that can slightly increase your yield as well as those that work against you. You verify your boxes with the field tally sheet, grab your now-empty buckets, and return to your rick to continue raking. A man may be able to carry four full buckets at once, but a 12-year old child will struggle to carry one.*

When Mr. Burns called lunchtime, I had filled almost half my bucket and was about halfway down my row. The Sunday school girls had all moved on, and the tall girl had just finished her row, mumbling, "Call me Molly" as she passed me by, or was it Holly? Everyone shuffled in from further afield to grab their lunches and to vie for spots in the shade cast by the truck. I was too slow to get a shady seat and had to make do with a spot that had shifting shadows cast by the straggly pines ringing the field. No one sat beside me and I tried to act like it didn't matter. My water was nearly gone and my bologna sandwich looked pathetically insufficient. I started with my apple, taking tiny bites that I hoped would trick me into feeling less hungry and thirsty. The apple was gone too soon and I was getting ready to eat the sandwich when I noticed the men from this morning's ride, the quiet one and the clowning one, looking at me. When I met their eyes, the funny one leapt to his feet and pulled the other one up.

"Whatcha doing sitting by yourself?" I looked up into the sun, shading my eyes with my hand and shrugged. He grinned, "Ah, a lady of mystery. I'm Mike. This is my cousin, Lester."

They dropped down in front of me and from close-up I realized they weren't as old as I'd thought this morning—more like much older high school boys. Mike had longish hair and brown eyes. He looked like he'd been dipped in honey, with everything from his hair to his skin shades of golden brown. He couldn't seem to sit still or stay quiet for very long, but Lester hadn't said a word. The silence was like a magnet, and I found myself studying him while Mike talked.

The crew boss came over, his disapproval palpable, and stood before the three of us. I felt myself shrinking, even though I wasn't sure what I'd done wrong.

"You didn't clear your rick. The rest of the crew is far enough along that I need to move the winnowing station. I want you to stay down here and finish your rick. When you've got it done, clean up the patches the other rakers missed. Leave your full buckets here when you're finished and walk down to where we are. I'll come back in the truck to pick them up while you start on a strip down there. Understand?" Misery settled over me as I nodded.

He turned his attention to Mike and Lester, squinting at them even though the sun wasn't in his eyes. "You boys behaving yourselves?"

Mike made his eyes wide and innocent, "We always do. Just saw someone sitting alone and thought it wasn't right to leave her all by herself like that. Being hospitable, like it says in the Bible, Mr.

Burns."

Lester had gone very still and looked at the crew boss with such hatred that I was confused and a little alarmed. "Yep," was all he said, the muscle in his jaw clenching and releasing.

The boss stood there another moment, sealing his authority, and then walked on.

"Well, that's no way to treat someone new, is it?" Mike asked brightly. "We'll stay and help you out, otherwise you'll be stuck down here all day. Right, Lester?"

Lester had been watching the crew boss walking off, and now swung his gaze over to me, trapping me. "Yeah," he said slowly. "Of course we will. Burns is a jerk to dump you down here like that. This is your first time, isn't it?"

"Yeah. It's a lot different than I thought it would be. Harder." I plucked at the feathery, dead-looking moss on the ground in front of me. He reached over and took it from me, his fingers brushing mine in a way that made me feel unsettled and strange.

"Reindeer moss." He shuffled it back and forth between his thumb and forefinger. "We use it wreathing. Deer eat it, too, if the winter's bad enough. Indians'll make tea out of it, but you have to be careful or it'll make you sick."

"I thought it was dead."

A fleeting smile passed across his face, showing small, regular teeth as white as the T-shirt he had neatly tucked into his jeans. I was aware of how dirty I'd managed to make my own T-shirt and shorts. Even my legs were streaked with dirt.

"Not dead. Just tough. This stuff," he held up the tuft of moss, "can grow even when the temps are below zero, and can live over a hundred years." He looked away, across the barren.

"There's a lot about the fields I never would've guessed at," I ventured. "Like how they smell. It's, um, it's intense. Not like blueberries smell when you eat them, but sort of spicy-sweet."

"That's the sweetfern." He stretched out to pluck some leaves from a dark, bushy plant

and I noticed the pale freckles across his upper arms and how his muscles shifted under the T-shirt. The scent I'd mentioned grew powerful as he brought the leaves back to where we were sitting, cross legged across from one another, our foreheads nearly touching. "It grows all over the barrens. Lots of what grows here can only grow here. This was all made when glaciers came down, leveling everything in their path, till they finally melted. That's what made the barrens. Those glaciers just scraped everything off right down to the granite and now only certain things can grow here ... but they can only grow here, you know? It's this amazing tradeoff that nature does, creating something unusable but at the same time making sure there's something special that can only work in that spot."

*Maine's unique landscape is the product of millions of years of hard wear by environmental forces, proving Renoir right when he said that pain passes but beauty remains. Glaciers, massive sheets of ice, rode down from the Arctic circle about twelve thousand years ago and scraped this ground down to granite bedrock. Some ice sheets were so massive that their weight caused the sea level to drop by as much as 500 feet. As the glaciers melted, the sands they'd dragged from other locations settled over these barren areas. Large chunks of ice were dropped and later melted, creating ponds and lakes called kettles. When you first see a barren, you may feel that you're looking at something unnatural, a set for a science fiction movie, perhaps. The ground is flat, but not uniformly so. The colors are subdued, other than in autumn when the palette defies description, so the blue of the berries looks contrived. You may not like the barrens when you stand on one; you may realize how brief and insignificant your contributions to the world actually are. On the other hand, this realization of transiency can be liberating. The barrens are nature at its most uncompromising. You are the creature that is out of place here, and nothing in your surroundings will soften that realization.*

Mike capered over. "Hey, I go off for a smoke and the next thing I know you guys are making the beast with two backs! No fair, Lester, you didn't even give me a chance!"

I felt hot as my skin turned red in a sudden, fiery blush. Mike laughed delightedly. "Look at her! She knows what I'm talking about!"

Lester scooted over and slung his arm over my shoulder. It was heavier than I expected. I was overwhelmed by so much, so new, happening so fast. The tangy, sweaty smell of him with undertones of some cologne overtook the heady fragrance of the sweetfern. His body radiated heat and where we were in contact, our knees touching and his arm over my shoulder, felt in danger of bursting into flame. This close to him, I could see the blueish shadow along his jawline and understood that he must shave daily. His ears were small pink seashells. His black, black hair was cut shorter in back and grew a little longer on top where the waves tousled over his forehead. His eyelashes were black and thick, making the dark blue of his eyes more intense. He had a squarish face with prominent cheekbones and the faintest spray of freckles over the bridge of his nose. In that instant, I committed him to memory for all time.

"Shut up, Mike. We're just talking. She's a good listener," he gently flexed his arm around my neck and for the first time, I felt that my quietness could actually be valued. He stood up and held a hand out to me; I looked at it for a long moment before I realized he was offering to help me up. I set my palm in his and he pulled me up and in toward him. Off balance, I stumbled and he smilingly set his free hand on my hip to steady me.

"Let's get busy, fellas!" he announced, taking his hands from me. "We've got to show old man Burns that he can't get the best of us."

That afternoon, I learned from Mike and Lester how to rake. Between Mike's constant clowning and Lester's intensity, the hours flew by. Mike shouted out dirty work songs that made me blush with embarrassment and Lester would quietly look over at me with his face serious but his eyes dancing. We zigzagged over that poor-quality end of the field, capturing every berry to be found with Mike offering commentary on how big the berries were compared to the crew boss' genitals. I laughed in spite of myself and caught another rare smile from Lester.

The boys carried the full buckets, four at a time, back to where the truck had been parked in the morning. I tried to help, staggering under the weight of a single bucket, but every time I lurched, berries fell out. Mike teased me about undoing all their hard work and took my bucket. As his cousin walked away, Lester leaned in and kissed me on the mouth. His lips were soft but

I remembered how hard his hands and arms felt earlier. Nothing but his mouth touched me now and I stared into the dark blue blur of his eyes, too near to see properly so he looked like a serious Cyclops. The thought made me smile, which broke the contact between our lips.

He touched his forehead to mine briefly, like a salute, and grabbed my hand to walk me over to where Mike was smoking and waiting with the full buckets.

Mike raised an eyebrow and waggled a finger at us. "I guess I know who gets to walk down to tell Burnsie we're all done here," he said, his voice both good-natured and a little mournful.

*When you strip a landscape of everything that is superfluous, those things which remain are interdependent upon one another. A necessity for connection is created. The commensalism of the barrens supports the rare plants and animals that grow here, but also leaves them vulnerable. A harm done to one ripples across the ecosystem, damaging all. Wild blueberry farmers have discovered this in their attempts to cultivate the barrens, such as ridding them of rocks only to discover that the natural pollinators relied on the rocky outcroppings for nests. Honeybees are now trucked in from southern states at great expense and additional ecological destruction, to keep the fields pollinated.*

*Nature creates us in such a way that we require contact, even though we are changed by it. The passage of the glaciers over this land, for example. You have learned how the ice sheets tore open and wore down the earth to create the barrens, but the glaciers were also broken and diminished in the process. The landscape created by their union is unlike anything you will find elsewhere on earth—bare boulders bigger than houses, kettle lakes of fresh blue water, deep deposits of purifying sand. You will learn that this is an ecosystem perfectly suited to support that which belongs there, and inhospitable to anything else.*

In the 80s, it wasn't unheard of to adjust school calendars to meet the needs of the harvest. We raked right up until school began, six days a week with church on Sunday. Lester sneaked down to the basement where the Sunday school classes were held to steal time with me. When he asked why I hadn't been at the upstairs service, that first Sunday after we met, I mumbled that I had to stay downstairs with the kids.

His eyes widened and then narrowed. "How old are you?" he breathed softly.

On the verge of tears, I admitted that I was only twelve. He stood very still and looked at me for a long while.

Finally, he reached out for a strand of my long hair and ran it over his fingers. "Well then. I guess I'll need to come downstairs to see you."

The night before school began, Lester called me. This first-ever call from a boy surprised my parents. I evaded their questions and used the confusion to my advantage by asking to use the phone in their bedroom instead of the one in the kitchen. Numbly, my mom nodded.

"Hey, it's me."

"Yeah, I noticed. You've turned my parents' world upside down," I laughed.

There was silence. I kept quiet, unsure if this was how phone calls between boyfriends and girlfriends were supposed to go. Finally, I asked if everything was okay.

"School's tomorrow, and, ah, there are things. I mean, I haven't told you everything." He sighed. "I don't know how to do this but just come out with it."

I heard a match scrape and his sharp inhalation. He smoked, but never around me. To smoke now must mean that something bad was about to happen.

"I killed someone a year ago and if people know you're with me, it's going to come up. People are going to say things. They're going to try to ruin this." His voice was low and angry, but also sad and tired. I held the receiver hard against my ear, as if the closer contact would make sense of the words.

"I guess I don't know what you're saying." I finally offered.

"Exactly what the words mean." His voice was flat. "I shot and killed a kid last year. I had to go to trial and everything. It was an accident." When he sighed, I could hear him shudder.

*You will be surprised to discover that the sweetfern is not a fern at all, but is a deciduous shrub. Its attractive presentation and heady aroma have attracted the attention of landscape gardeners. However, attempts to successfully cultivate it outside of its native habitat have proven frustrat-*

ing to experts. Blueberry growers, on the other hand, have been frustrated by the tenacity of the shrub, which stubbornly dots even the most carefully tended barrens. Sweetfern seeds, after laying dormant in the soil for as long as seventy years, require ideal exposure to strong temperature fluctuations. These intense fluctuations tell the seed that full sun is once again available and that if it germinates now, it is likely to flourish. This plant is uniquely suited to its environment, passing up the enriched soils of show gardens for hardy survival on the blueberry barren.

"Tell me about it," I said, my voice soft.

## Storyteller

When the summer sun had warmed the soil,
I found the hard-shelled pupa of a Sphinx moth.
The Passamaquoddy elder had told me its story.

As his grandmother had shown him, he held
the shiny brown creature between his thumb and finger.
The pupa moved its segmented tail—sideways for "no."
He asked another question.
The pupae moved again, this time
up and down for "yes."

Many mysteries lie waiting under the crust of a winter garden.
Something like magic rises out of the dark, silent earth
that has long been fertilized with old fish and clam shells.
Here the taste of story begins.

—Leslie Wood

# Hardware Store, Bar Harbor

I buy some rough-whiskered rope, sturdy-
in-its-strands rope to lift a mainsail,
to lift a jib. Rope good enough for lashing.
Rope perfect for practicing: fisherman's
knot, reef knot, square knot to bind everyone
to everyone else, grapple-hitch that takes
me everywhere I mean to go, clove-hitch
that forever keeps approaching reconciliation.
I even like to make up knots: the un-
assailable knot, the not-me knot.
A decent length of twine is all I need to loop
a slew of slip knots. One tug from both ends
at once: human undoing.

—Grey Held

## The Hill

When I think of my dad I think of this hill
in Brewer, Maine steep as the roof of an A-frame
just before you turn onto the Airline to Calais

where if you're driving manual you wish it
was automatic, wish you were where you're
heading which for him was back to the mill

in Woodland, clutching the crest of this hill
every weekend all winter, back from Boston
easing it out, accelerating, mouth full of No-Doz.

Nothing to it; everything to it. Most of which
I will never know. I'm just puttering through
another summer on my way to Cobscook

where an eagle will rise from its nest and drop
one worn white feather into the reversing
current as I paddle over jellyfish pulsing

like crazy flowers above urchins and stars
that cling to the kelp covered ledges,
clearly at home in the ocean's deep cold.

—Susan Johnson

# The Descent into Harvey

In Vanceboro, the customs lady beamed
from her booth, asked about firearms.
Shocked, stammering my innocent truth,
I fled across the border.
In McAdam, two boys, in their
own backyard, played catch without noise.

In twilight, suddenly, Harvey appeared below:
white houses, gray-peaked roofs alike,
wreathed in murky, loose array
along both sides of the
downward curve of the still, empty road
and, opposite, dimly adorned another hill.

Lurching upward, the road veered out
of town. Fast, in the mirror
I stole a dusky last
peek, and gave to those
who know home here thoughts wrenched
from a habitat elsewhere and mere.

—Robert J. Ward

# March Hill

Old timers count who has not crossed March Hill,
the crest of a long winter before the short
downslope into spring. Pneumonia,
the old man's friend, claimed
the fortunate flu victim before
the first hard freeze. Later corpses wait,
the wooden men caught in the woods,
the woman who forgot to load the stove.

Winter's hard work buys the etched spot
on parchment skin, collapsed lungs
devoid of moisture, a frozen stare that
eases in June. Those left dread October,
treasure long summer days in farm fields,
expect next winter to catch them
like a low forgotten eave on which
you bang your head and realize
loss as you fall into eternity.

It's a long climb from October to April,
made harder by snow afoot, ice overhead.
By the time the bear comes out to grind your bones
on the far side of March Hill, all the rest of you
is warm somewhere else.

—Michael R. Brown

# Hawk's View

A sea sweep of green leaves
as above so below and we gaze and gaze
no one speaks
   goldfinch and cardinal
thrill the air their crimson yellow flits
now the breeze stirs and maples
wave to moving oaks
we left behind the measured miles
   the curbed and metered walks
here no price rules
    river flows
    forest grows
  as below so above
don't tell me there is no love

—Patrick Gentry Pierce

# Bill

Cynthia Huntington

It's a complicated story, I hope I don't leave anything out. It began years ago when I met Bill and his wife, Marion, at an antique car show. They were in their 70's. He was unmistakably native. My mother's family claims to be part Penobscot. I don't look the part, but then a lot of us don't. Actually, now that I think about it, on my father's side there is even a mulatta grandmother. There is no last name on her headstone, just "Sara the mulatta." I have always hoped that someone loved her. It is very sad to think of an ancestor as being unloved or worse, just chattel, a vehicle whose only function is to satisfy someone else's needs.

Anyway, Bill and I became friends. Marion became my friend also. For a long time I thought she was the person I was supposed to meet, but as it turned out that was not the case.

Bill became very ill the first year we met. I drove Marion to the hospital often to visit him. On one occasion, while working in my garden putting up poles for the beans, I decided to stop what I was doing and make Bill a medicine bag. The thought just hit me from out of nowhere, and within minutes there I was saying prayers and gathering things for the medicine bag. I did a good job. The bag itself was made of rabbit skin—from a rabbit that had been shot two winters ago. I keep the skins in my freezer until I am ready to treat them. Then I just take out what I need and leave the rest frozen. The drawstring was made from a strip of rawhide. I put a number of small and potent things in the bag, but the strongest of all was an exquisite fossil of a feather my mother found on Mt. Katahdin when she was a girl. My Mother had the sight. She found things or they found her. Fossils nearly jumped out at her. She had given me four or five of them years ago before she died. It is not my

84

way to hold on to things. Things have a life of their own and often need to go somewhere else. Over the years when it felt right I had given away some of the fossils. Some went to my grandchildren—this one was meant for Bill. During the weeks that followed Bill kept the medicine bag with him all the time. It would rest on the bed next to him or on very bad days hang from the pole that held his IV. Eventually he got better and went home.

Then something changed. There was a shift in our friendship, Marion came by less, but Bill visited more often. We talked about things. Often after he left I would think more about what had not been said than what was. He talked a lot about his native Choctaw culture. Me, I always felt at a loss, a bit ignorant not being raised to it as he had. We also laughed a lot. He was so good at seeing through the inconsistencies of society. He would point out foolishness with just a few well-placed words or a casual gesture.

When Bill got sick again a few years later he did not bring his medicine bag to the hospital with him. When I went to visit him I would look around the room to see if it was there, but I never asked. I didn't feel it was my place.

Marion was angry. Bill had told her he was dying and she behaved as though it was his last act of defiance—you know—dying? She was full of rage. She screamed at the doctors and social workers. She insisted he was not dying, he was just depressed and that if he would only think positively all would be well. If he would just put his mind to it then he would come home and they could continue to drive to yard sales and go to lunch. Marion loved to lunch out. When I took her to the hospital to visit with Bill she always insisted on stopping for lunch even though it often took more time than I had. She would insist, and I would give in, knowing she missed doing this.

Bill said to me a few weeks before he died, "I am dying and if ever there was a time I needed that woman to listen it is now." But every time he said, "I am dying," she would respond with, "Oh, no you're not, you just need to eat more … get more rest … come home … just think positive." And I could feel Bill pull back into himself as he lay there in bed, eyes closed, wishing she would just leave the room. I stopped bringing her with me after that.

So, on March 9th I went to the hospital to see Bill and he asked me to hold his hand. I sat with him for hours like that. Sometimes he would talk about his grandfather who had walked The Trail of Tears as a child. One time he said, "It is good to know you are here. It is good to not have to talk."

I went back the next day. He was very weak, and I sat with him without speaking, just holding his hand. I had brought a native tape with me as I had seen the day before that there was a radio/cassette player on the table by his bed. We listened to White Buffalo Woman and The Beauty Trail and many other songs of our people and it was good to sit with my friend and know that we did not have to talk and that he would go where he wanted unhindered by words or someone else's will.

We sat that way a long time and sometime way into the night the doctor came and checked him. I asked how long Bill could stay like that, between two worlds, and he said he did not know, hours, maybe weeks. And then I did something that I had not planned it just seemed like the right thing, the only thing. The tape was playing and the native drums gave rhythm and purpose to my hands as I reached for his left ear and pulled gently at the air. As the movement of my hands became one with the sound of the drumming I began to feel tension in the air that I was pulling from his ear. So help me, it felt like a nylon stocking being stretched gently to its limit and then slowly withdrawing back into his ear. Finally, after a few tries I pulled it free then brought my hands up to my lips and blew gently across my palms. I sat with him in the room for a while longer listening to the music before I went to get the nurse.

I have not felt like myself since then. I am tired and have begun taking naps occasionally in the afternoon. I, too, am waiting to dream.

## After *El Faro*

Were it my only sister
fed to the sea, (or swallowed
by clambering cancer cells,
or found in a deathly doze
three hundred miles away
in her cat-clawed wingback chair),

when the unwanted arrives
packaged in tears,
will my distress
skim the surface
like a rainy-day road
that dries overnight,

or, when the unseemly
screams for justice
will grief surge
as a hurricane-wrought
Atlantic that rocks itself
even in the calm?

Will I sorrow more
for absence of presence
or for singular rememberings,
fingered one by one
dangling like fringe
on the afghan she crocheted:

bread pudding with raisins
in Momma's poppy bowl,

the scraping in the cellar
when Dad shoveled coal,

newspaper for a blanket
while napping on the floor?

Why mourn at all, I ask,
for that which cannot be retrieved,
the sunken and the void; yet,
plunge we must into depths of loss
until comfort seeps within,
and saturates the marrow.

—Grace Sheridan

Jazz trumpet wind
is wailing hard enough to
blow stars from the sky.

—Danielle Woerner

# The Rosary

*for Mary Lillian (Doucette) Surette*

I

"He's not going to say the whole goddamn thing,"
groaned Sonny, and his peers moaned with him.
But say it he did, fingering the beads—
Apostles' Creed, Our Father,
Hail Mary's and Glory Be's,
Twenty mysteries.

He's a good grandson.
He said it for her,
claimed she said one every day of her life,
a devotion born with her naming—
shared with seven sisters, all Mary's—
she the sole survivor.

II

She and I watched the Bruins together.
86 games and in the good years—playoffs.
Bucyk to Bourke
into her nineties, still sharp,
though she began to count replays as additional goals.

She kept score in a spiral notebook—
no personal insights—just goals and games.
I never saw her hold those beads or say a prayer.
We never talked of God, Jesus or the Pope.
But I knew Kenny Hodge was her all-time favorite,

and she liked red heads because she would sigh
when Glen Wesley took off his helmet.

And when she talked of Raymond her accent tilted to French.

III

The last decade was called. And we had answered.
But I wanted Fred to do the Eulogy with color by Derek.
I wanted one more time for her to see a replay and ask,
"Did we score again?"
I wanted all the Mary's gathered
to skate around her coffin.

—David R. Surrette

## Fact of Fate

My auto missed hitting a doe's flank this
morning, and after I could not eat.
Driving off I saw a rising sun's rays glance off
a setting moon's cheeks,
the heavenly bodies steady, on course.
Bound to earth, I whispered I love you to them
and to what I could pick out leaping beyond the
road in fields and woods, hungry for life.

—Mark Melnicove

# a mere geometry of light

Some days I can't materialize.
    No brave boat
        no warship     no pirate's

vessel. I can more easily imagine my life
    as a work of sorcery
        one more witch

of the wrack line
        singing *climb down to me.*
Haven't I always been complicated?

     Imitating the things I hate
        erecting castles I know are doomed
  to be scaled

        and overturned.
Don't dare dismiss me—your fata morgana—
     I am just like you   made up

mostly of water    hushing  *goodbye*
  *purple sailor*        *velella velella*
    another great colony lost to the tide.

I have no good reason for the days
     I rise out of the blue
      and sing a little tune of sea/self/sky:

another doubtful trinity. The deep wavering

of reckoning myself up.

*Opening*

like the mouth of the baleen,
            its ragged threads blindly filtering
        whatever enters

I am sustained
        by the tiniest things.      I am composed
    almost entirely            of unraveling.


—Wendy Cannella

# Winter Madness

Don't want no blood and gore,
No au courant trash—Flash,
My name is Flash, I run
Glazed streets in a white suit.
Owner of a heart of stone
Quarried Downeast,

On a smoky March day
The north wind rides my shoulders.
Don't get too close, that wind's
Breathing down my neck.

Gotta mirror in my pocket,
Want to see what you look like
With a hangnail?
Touch me with that finger,
You'll never hear the ice crack.

Never mind, I see a raven turning south
And the coffee's getting cold.

—Bunny L. Richards

## Facing Both East & West at the Same Time
### Along Passamaquoddy Shores

1.
This story comes through nights with gnawing in the walls
Bobcat tracks to the hens.
Last stored cabbages and squash.
Below-zero weeks-after-weeks when trucks are safe
on the ponds and lakes and tides and light right
for muslins and rice paper prints of petroglyphs down at Machias Bay.

21y.
This story is drug from winter's huddling.
The drive to get out, sniff the air, collect signs
in order to bear winter's last grip before sap
commences its tidal tum. This story rises three thousand
years Before Present, up through fire, silt, and salt
all the way from first people pecking into stone
to a woman shocking with her cell phone ordering pizza
from the gallery as if from church to be picked up after prayer.

3ly.
This story takes ages to tell after mere hours to arrive
over coastal curves treacherous with black ice to the place.
This story bears reverence at once. Then, and again.
And however many agains its knowledge is sought
the way sopping figures appear and disappear through kelp.

41y.
In the hall is a book going with this timeless story
where those privileged to enter its presence draw
how they want to be kept in history for having come.
Some simply ink their names. Others, the spirit

of early representation, *This is my hand.... my tribe....*
*This is the center of our world..... This is where I've*
*come from....my position....what I know....*
*I was here.... Thank you...tears....* But we
are not chiseled in stone and will soon be gone.

5ly.
This sacred history saved in round time by Hedden
(the teacher with a name seasoned as a woodpile)
has been shown with tribal blessings by Vinzani
(the teacher with sizzling logs in his name),
burning their marks here from coals deep within
the carved rocks where the Passamaquoddy ancestors live.
We know this because of the teachers Nicholas, Francis, Newell,
Soctomah, and other wisdom keepers whose names witness
how the blood of the artists who made the petroglyphs
still runs strong in their people whose ancient home this is.

6ly.
Caught in this fire and centrifugal force, a figure no one notices
(on the bench in the middle) bows for understanding.
No one can see the black fur down her neck, spray
of porcupine crown, dissident protestant chain.
She shivers from the likenesses of the shamanic glyphs
to magnified genes. And the *heaven and below* symbol
to the pattern of chromosomes bearing undeniable inscriptions.

The print from the gouged out European ship and cross
shows her a truth: she is both on the ship looking West
(and all that means), and on the land watching East
(and all that means). Both, afraid. No wonder
her muscles twist, turning both directions at once. No wonder
she can't forget all that is mixed in her heart aching to unite.

7ly.
Home (in the night), she finds these figures floating
in spiral visions and patterns on her dreams,
the portion of The People still in her
(every ninth and tenth star and then some)
eroding and crumbling away each generation,
sorrow and shame weighting the wonder
(the seaweed and depths keep hidden from most).
But the searchers who follow inscribed revelations
(treading softly across her being on earth) know
what they are finding until the water level  rises
to the point when what is left drawn on her bones
pulls away in the undertow,
crushes into sand and whispers (at last) (with the others)
in the grain of those who saw (and  knew).

```
*                       *      *
*          *                   *      *
    *                *
      *
```

8ly.
The woman to whom this has been shown
has put it down in the old numerical form of "treating minutes"
reported in Richter's history, *Facing East From Indian Country,*
her arms in the giving back position,
her feet (at long last) facing (again) in the same direction on stone.

—Patricia Smith Ranzoni

# My Mother and the Adze

Frances Drabick

While walking along the water on Passamaquoddy Bay, my partner noticed a smooth stone sticking out like a tongue from the ground. She pulled it out. It was a stone adze with three quarter-inch carved slash-marks on the cutting-end. It was about 6.5" long, 2" at its widest point, and 1.5" wide at its cutting edge. Its cutting edge was smooth, sharp, and looked like it had just been polished.

On seeing it, I thought of my mother's roots stemming from the tribe she had talked about all of my growing years. The Susquehannock Tribe that she spoke of were located along the Susquehanna River in Pennsylvania where both sets of my mother's family settled. They were mostly Scots and High Swiss that married and formed American generations since the early to mid-1770s when they emigrated.

I was fascinated with the adze, and decided to read more about the Susquehannock settlements along the Atlantic Coast in *Diversity and Complexity in Prehistoric Maritime Societies: A Gulf of Maine Perspective*, by Bruce J. Bourque.

To my amazement, on page 245 was a photo of a broken adze with the same three carved markings on one end. I realize it could well be the stone maker's mark.

The adze in the book was found in an archaeological dig on North Haven island in Penobscot Bay. But what truly stunned me was this heading on page 244: *The Susquehanna Tradition North and South*. More headings followed about the Susquehanna tradition. I had no idea that a Susquehanna "tradition" had been so widespread, and had also been here in Maine. My mother only spoke of Pennsylvania. According to the book, the Susquehannock appeared suddenly in Maine around 4000–3800 B.P. and *"suddenly disappeared before 3500 B.P. possibly resulting in regional depopulation."*

I was so excited with this information about my mother's heritage being so near to where I settled, that I called the author of the book for confirmation.

Traces of my mother's ancestral tribe were found in archaeological digs at Turner Farm, located on North Haven Island in Penobscot Bay. Artifacts and burials of the Susquehanna Tradition were dating to the Age of Occupation 3, from 4020–3105 B.P. and spanned more than a millennium. *"The earliest date is on carbonized wood from a cremation."*

When we buried my mother in Upstate New York in 1992, I kept a yellow rose from her funeral wreath. For years, I thought about where to bury it or perhaps place it in the sea. Fate was working with me when my mate introduced me to a woman who was born, raised, and lived on North Haven. As a child, she played at Turner Farm, the site of the archaeological digs. We told her about the adze we found and the one in the book which shared the same markings and must have come from the same Age of Occupation 3. There was evidence of my mother's tribe at Turner Farm.

She gave us a private tour of the island. On quiet ground I buried my mother's rose. Finding the adze led me here. I know my mother would have been pleased to make a connection to her ancestors.

## They Could Be Stars

In dark suspension, oracles in jeweled turbans
coo their prophecies into the dusty weather
of this old barn's vaulted chamber.

It's so drab in here, a tenement
for rats and owls. Bats lisp unharmoniously.
They are immune to the beauty of the sun.

Pinhole after pinhole dots the ceiling.
They have been here forever, euthanizing
their children, and are old pros at this sort of thing.

Dust motes float in weeping rods of light;
they could be stars dropping their luminesces
from the tiny pinpoints overhead.

Each spotlight was born from a different story;
each shingle loosened and fallen like a bad tooth.
Back then their lives were less important.

In the blue air above the stars, birds go
about their business, chattering like children
in a park, oblivious to the night trappings here.

—Caroline Misner

# Welcome to Great Village

Ellie O'Leary

When I started a project studying New England women writers, their houses and home areas, I knew narrowing it down to just one on the long list of over thirty wouldn't be easy. Elizabeth Bishop and I both grew up in rural villages on the North American side of the Atlantic, she in Nova Scotia and me in Maine. We both suffered early childhood parental loss and both had a maternal aunt who was a strong role model. I realized she was where I best begin.

On May 1st, I headed to Great Village, Nova Scotia to attend a board meeting of the Elizabeth Bishop Society. Before this trip, I had been in contact with Sandra Barry, biographer, who had also been President of the Board. When she invited me to the meeting I initially hoped that I wouldn't be intruding but then decided I'd be foolish not to attend. I was, after all, invited. There were about half a dozen of us in attendance in a family home. These people didn't know me, but they were gracious. I was handed a nice pile of what could be called Elizabeth Bishop bling including some pencils, a refrigerator magnet, and a post card. When I admired a book of winning entries for a writing contest a few years ago, the hostess said, "Oh would you like it? Please keep it." They also hunted down and handed me a copy of a walking tour of Great Village. I was feeling grace from them and gratitude from me.

Going along with the agenda for the meeting I heard the standards—old business and the treasurer's report. I'm the executive director of a non-profit that teaches first time homebuyer workshops. I'm familiar with board meetings. In this one I planned to alternate between making polite conversation and keeping my mouth shut. I did, until they got to "outside business."

"That would be you, Ellie."

At first I felt my mind go blank; then it reset and booted up again. They wanted to hear about my project and I hoped I wouldn't come across as a complete neophyte on the topic of Bishop. I explained that I had a list (actually it's an extensive spreadsheet) of New England women writers. Lovely, I thought. I just called their Nova Scotia poet a New England writer. I explained that I had narrowed it down to a few, but decided to start with Elizabeth Bishop because I, too, grew up in a village.

"We had a pond, not an ocean. Also, just as she on occasion had pretended her mother was dead, I had pretended mine was alive."

I figured that was far enough, if not too far, into the personal connection I felt with Bishop, except that I did tack on that I was living in Boston in October 1979 when Bishop died there. I decided not to mention that my ex-husband is from Worcester and so I have been there on a number of occasions. We all agreed the Maritime Provinces and the New England states have much in common, although they reminded me that for them New England is also known as the Boston States. I mentioned that there were people in Maine who would not be pleased to hear that.

They went on to discuss the AMG, which at first I did not understand, but it turned out to be the Annual General Meeting to be held in June at the now decommissioned Presbyterian church, which operates as a community center and café during the warmer months. It was not open during my visit. The guest speaker at the AMG would be Emma FitzGerald who lives in Halifax but has visited sites relating to Bishop in Brazil. I thought my trip to Nova Scotia was a big deal.

As the meeting was breaking up, I mentioned that I would be driving home in the morning. Sandra asked me if I would be following the tides. I think that's what she asked but what she said next eclipsed that.

"Are you going along 'The Moose' route? "

"The moose route?"

"Yes, this road right here in front of the house. That's the route in the poem.

"That's the way the bus went?"

"Yes, just go along 2. Follow the signs to Amherst."

"Follow Route 2 to Amherst? Funny, that would also be the way to Emily Dickinson's house, from where I live."

The following morning instead of getting on the larger highway towards New Brunswick and home, I went through the village once more. I drove down the narrow road to the cemetery. It's a simple, retreat-like setting compared to other graveyards I've visited. There are no tall monuments, no bigger-than-life angel statues, and no ornate stone crosses. There are engraved headstones in rows in this place at the end of the road, overlooking the bay. I found the Bulmer grandparents' stone and said a few words to them. I have often thought how miserable it must have been for them to surrender their Elizabeth to her Worcester grandparents after losing their daughter to mental illness.

After this final stop, I headed along Highway 2 towards Amherst, Nova Scotia. The bay was on my left for miles, the color of deep water, not the red sand color of low tide from a few days before. The place names came at me from out of "The Moose." I drove through Bass River and the Economies, laughing to myself that Central Economy, as it said on the sign, sounded more like the title of a policy statement than the name of a place. After I passed through Five Islands, Highway 2 took me north towards Amherst. These working-class towns reminded me of Central Maine. These are the places real working people, year-long residents, have populated for generations. While I did see some beautiful views, these are not the picturesque tourist spots of brochures and websites.

I did not encounter a moose as Bishop's bus ride did in the poem, but shortly after crossing back into New Brunswick along the side of multi-lane, divided Highway 1—just behind the guardrail—I saw a doe and her fawn. They were casually munching grass, seemingly oblivious to traffic noise or that anyone passing by might try to make a poetic, maternal moment of them.

## Thinking Potatoes

French Fingerlings. Magic Molly.
In a shallow box by the window
this year's tubers warm to the thought
of growing. They understand fertility
as a sequence of moves. Fuzzy sprouts
push from the dust-shriveled skin,
eyes urge toward an opening.

Obliging, I will place each tuber
into the soil of their dark-days
like others before me—a line of planters
who have bent over shallow trenches,
who have hilled and watered
and in summer marveled at elegant plants
bearing white and purple blooms.

The strength of these earth companions—
to burrow down and resurrect.
In the Andes, the world-mother is offered
a meal and a sprinkling of *chicha*.
Does she fathom the depth of our hunger?
Cradled in my hand, this nightshade
offers something like a future.

—Leonore Hildebrandt

## Observations on the Garden, Fourth of July

As pole beans bottle rocket bursting buds
        Into the horizon of chicken wire, suddenly
I marvel at the fireworks of my beloved veggies
        Celebrating this great, green diverse nation
Where Southern collards abide neighboring
        Yankee broccoli—while Waspy, sweet corn aids
Humble pole beans seeking like Wall Street
        Heights. And when the Italian squash explode
Their blooms' M-80's, I see my immigrants' zeal
        In moving from greenhouse indentured servitude
To thriving in their high-rise, raised bed homes—
        So that now I'm the Founding Father of this garden
Who brilliantly scribed the constitution of compost pile
        And polices the fenced-in borders for raiding
Woodchucks and tunneling skunks. Oh MLK
        Would set off a firework of words if taking in
My companion planting's seamless integration
        Of black bean beside white carrot! And Hamilton,
I think, would admire our green-leafed currency
        Always backed by the gold standard of organic
Seeds! Tomorrow, then, I'll wake early to resume
        This Westward expansion over the Great Plains
Of half-acre field where not one native burdock
        Or hollyhock is exterminated. And nights, I'll scribe
A State of the Union calling for all patriotic produce
        "To imagine a nation where each humble pea
Has access to a trellis and our much praised
        Upward mobility." And planting myself deep

Into the dirt of service to my people,
            May I create a legislative body of loam
Perfectly balancing the two major parties
            Of acid and alkaline so that all feel
Their congress of roots can thrive.
            And may the history book of garden log praise
How we overcame the Pearl Harbor
            Of Japanese beetles raiding our island nation
Soon after we fought the Huns of woodchucks
            On foreign soil before their tanks in-
Filtrated our burgeoning cities of kale.
            Now, though, time for some of Jefferson's wine
And to just let my people put up their rooves
            Of blooms and split shingles of leaves—
While the pioneering pumpkins and cucumbers
            Fulfill our manifest destiny in wheeling
The covered wagon trains of their leaves
            Through the Rockies of wild blackberries
And, tomorrow, I finally recognize the beacon
            We're becoming to all oppressed seedlings
By placing a great torch in the scarecrow's hand
            To call forth every immigrant kernel adrift
In the ocean of breeze (or stowed in the vole's
            Furry hold) to choose this greatest of lands
From seed to shining seed.

—Dennis Camire

# Smithy

*For Arthur E. Hill*

Fire's out, forge decayed
coal and iron spent,
shop's song silent
as tires and tarps
press out old days
and horses who'd wait
for farrier to fettle
their feathered feet.
But fired and proved,
his Peter Wright Patent
solid wrought anvil rests
still on an oak stump
cut off winter's wood.
Vertical grain inspired
a spring and ring,
its own centurion hymn:
the swayed face,
chisel edges chipped,
horn and heel pocked
by hammer strikes
on shoes our horses wore
level with toes rolled fair.

Learned in all skills
known to smithies past,
he flowered in iron,
bent steel to be
in flat open furnace,
air forced through coal
orange hot in fire pot.

Scarred leather chaps flapped
betwixt horse and hearth,
each hoof nipped, measured, fit:
tools echoed a rhythmic clang,
embers glowed with bar stock
cut on hardy sharp,
a shower of sparks,
blow by blow;
steel bent, pritchel punched,
heels filed smooth
and water cooled.
A strong, deft touch
drove every nail point true,
straight side out,
into a living wall;
clinched, rasped, dressed
silver slippers made one by one,
his work now done.

—Andrea Suarez Hill

# Smelting

Sharon Mack

Even though Sewall is expecting me, when I arrive at his Pleasant River fish shack, he is squatting in the bushes outside, pants around
his ankles, with a roll of toilet paper in his hand. It's a warm February
morning but I'm sure he feels a chill wind. I keep right on driving the
car past his position and circle around the dirt road, giving him time to
right himself.

The smelts are running, the tide is high in the cove and
Sewall — a little bit comedian, a lot crusty old Mainer, and a lifelong fisherman — is holding court at Columbia Falls. Almost 75 years old, Sewall
is a thin man, skinny with knobby joints, a hoary beard, and skin beaten
dark from a lifetime of working outside on the sea. He welcomes me, a
stranger seeking to learn about smelting, but doesn't mention our earlier encounter of the bushes.

Sewall is the patriarch of the smelt camps here, the last com-
mercial smelt fishery on the Eastern Coast of the United States, and due
to his seven decades of experience, he has earned the unspoken title
of King of the Downeast Smelters. "I've been smelting since I was 14,"
Sewall says. I watch him talk while he peers out the front of the smelt
shack towards the river and ice, keeping a close eye on the comings and
goings of other fishermen and the sprinkling of ice shacks in the cove.

I can hear the call of sea ducks and the rush of the river in the
few places it is open. Every once in a while I hear a loud burst of laughter
from one of the ice shacks. For these smelters, it is their summer camp in
the winter — a place to bond and laugh and fish.

"I knew the run had started the other day when I saw nine mer-
gansers diving in the open water," he says. I am in awe of this ability to
know the ways of water, this knowledge of how it slides over rocks and
bellies into sandy holes. Where the rocks cause turns and twists, and

110

how the tides change the flow. I once knew a farmer who accurately predicted weather by smelling the air. He would look at a perfectly blue sky and tip his head and say "Rain should start around four." He was always within a half hour of calling it perfectly. Sewall's water instinct must be like that.

Sewall's fish shack sits in a short row of similar shacks in various states of seediness, wasted and weakened by old age and harsh weather. Sewall's is a narrow box of roughness—both inside and out. It is dressed in curled and weathered cedar shingles on all sides and its roof. Bare boards and beams inside, planks covering the floor. A trio of scavenged, mismatched windows allows us to see if someone is coming from the west, as well as watch the ice to the east. The fish shack is set close to the riverbank and is nearly surrounded by water at high tide. Sewall has put an old wooden ladder across a particularly wet spot, between the bank and the ice, that we and other smelters on the river can use as a boardwalk.

Sewall and I sit and talk about the river and the smelt, with me doing most of the listening. Sewall is a happy man here on this water and the stories of smelting bubble and flow from him easily. He's like a pitcher on the mound, a chef at the stove, a taxi driver on familiar streets. This is where he belongs.

Sewall hauls his thin frame up from his ancient, shabby recliner to take a closer look at the tide chart.

"Today is the fifth, right?" he asks no one in particular. "It's gonna be a high riding tide, boys. Ten feet, seven. They're gonna run good." He peers again at the cove, squinting and causing the lines around his eyes to become even deeper as the reflection of the winter sunshine makes the ice appear even whiter than it is.        "The smelts come upstream on the high tide, lay their eggs and go back to the sea as the tide ebbs," he says.

At dawn that morning, Sewall placed two 75-foot nets vertically in the cove, under the ice. He drilled a hole, floated the net in, and then—because he knows that cove like the back of his own hand-drilled a second hole, pulled up the other end of the net and secured it.

He puts both hands on his skinny hips, elbows high. "When I pull that net in today, boys, I look for it to be all silver."

I'm flooded with sadness for this old man. He is trying to keep a Downeast tradition alive that is dying before his very eyes and he knows he is losing. The fisheries are barren; the fish factories are shuttered and crumbling. Just like his beloved silvery-green smelts, Sewall is a dying breed.

He sighs long and slow. He looks to the water, lost in the memories of waters teeming with smelt. "There was so much smelt that we sold them, we used them for bait, we ate them, and then we threw the extras on our fields as fertilizer," Look says.

But rainbow smelt are in trouble and for reasons not largely understood. Look says some streams that once hosted millions of migrating smelts, host none. "Empty as a fart," he says.

Look holds his gnarled hands out in front of him and looks at them as if they are strangers. He tells me that he packed hundreds of wooden boxes filled with smelt as a teenager. "When I first started catching with Fat Oliver—he's long dead—we would pack them head to tail, head to tail, and then bring them to the train station and ship 'em to Boston. I asked Fat Oliver how much we would get paid and he said we'd have to wait for the check to come. That's how it was done then."

A smile creeps up his aged face as he tells a tale of once harvesting 360 pounds from one net. He pauses as if a newsreel of that catch is playing in his head.

"Yesterday, I got ten pounds," he says quietly. Sewall now has but a handful of customers, mostly friends and neighbors, who come down to the fish camp to buy the fresh smelts and sit a spell.

The wood stove pushes the camp past 82 degrees. Sewall opens the door to let the sunshine in and the overheated air out. This camp is where all the discarded furniture left by the side of the road go to their final end. There are recliners whose fabric is worn so thin that I can't really tell what they are made of, an orange sofa, a blue wing chair, an office chair with metal arms and a garden seat. Oars are stored in the rafters and a cast iron frying pan and spatula hang close by the wood stove. Totes full of nets are stacked in a corner, awaiting repair. Bags of silvery fish sit on a wooden counter.

The camp has heat but little else besides the jumble of seats. It is lighted with camping lanterns and hands are washed outside in the briny water. I am keenly aware there is no bathroom. I'm introduced to Abby, a fat white dog that follows Sewall everywhere. Abby moves back and forth from a tattered chair by the wood stove to the sunny deck facing the water, greeting every new visitor, and by lunchtime, I feel the atmosphere change.

The quiet of this shabby retreat evaporates as it transforms into a gathering place. Visitors start arriving. They are all men, and nearly every one brings three cold beers: one for themselves, one for Sewall, and a spare for Sewall's cooler. It's a parade of retirees— old fishermen, old sardine packers, old truck drivers. They buy fish in zippered plastic bags to take home. Sewall takes the old frying pan down from the wall and removing one fish from each sold bag, he begins cooking. The smelts are coated in cornmeal and they sizzle and pop on the wood stove. When the fish is cooked, Sewall wraps them in newspaper—a fish shack take-out. It seems every one of his guests has a story to share. A big burly guy named Poke talks about fishing and hunting. Lester brags about his new truck. Sewall weighs in on each topic. The men are respectful that "there is a lady present," as Sewall says, and they keep the jokes clean and their swearing to a minimum.

"On weekends, there is no place to sit," Sewall tells me. "It's beer and smelts and killin' time."

Sewall launches into a humorous rendition of his rescue last fall from cold waters off Plummet Island. "We was hand lining for cod," he says. The boat began taking on water and the captain pushed her as fast as he could towards a nearby island. They nearly made it when the boat sunk. "They put two life preservers on me and a life ring round my neck," Sewall recalls. He says that when he spotted the rescue boat "it looked soooooo far away." He was hauled unceremoniously out of the water and placed by the boat's heater. Sewall says that when he stopped shaking enough to speak, he told his rescuer "You are the prettiest thing I've ever seen." Sewall says he saw the man the next day at a local gas station. "How do I look today?" the captain asked. "As ugly as always," Sewall answered.

The afternoon lazes on with visitors rotating through the chairs. The frying pan never gets cool. These men are so comfortable with each other. There is no tension when the talking and

113

laughing cease for a few minutes and all is quiet, save for the occasional squawk of a duck. I feel almost cocooned, transported to another place and another time yet one that has existed for centuries.

Sewall tells another joke. Lester chimes in with one of his own. The men in the camp laugh and slap their knees. Sewall puts another log in the wood stove and once again checks the tide chart. "Yup. I'll pull those nets about one o'clock," he decides. "Then we'll see what we have."

# Big Fish Story

## J. C. Elkin

It was an historic event: the last submarine launch at the Portsmouth Naval Ship Yard in New Hampshire—or Maine, depending on who you ask. Truth often straddles the line that way, and such shades of verity still colored my family's recollection thirty years later. We were five people remembering five versions of the same event.

We watched the christening from a hundred feet away, all except my father, who was on the launch team and told us where to dash for the best view once the gates opened to the public. We stood on a seawall opposite the launch ramp with a clear view of the boat's port bow as she was readied to slide down the ways into the churning, black abyss. Locals liked to brag that stretches of the Piscataqua, the defining geographic feature of our town, had the seventh strongest current in the world, though no one could point to that fact in a book.

I knew it was summer, 1970. It had to be, based on the fact that it was a weekday with no school and I was wearing the striped cut-offs that were my favorite the summer I was ten. Some people bookmark recollections with news stories, others with a calendar in their head, but my reference point has always been wardrobe. Memory is strange that way.

The boat was one of those subs named for a big fish: the *Dolphin*, I thought. I stared at its bulk for an hour, its weight growing with each Sousa march the band tootled from the grandstand. The grey vessel looked ominous and anonymous as The Red Scare. It was huge. So huge, in fact, it was hard to imagine how it would fit in the narrow channel issuing from the boathouse without swamping the surrounding land. Even at age ten, simple bathtub physics told me the water would overflow the embankment and soak us all. Maybe even drown us.

I tried to warn my mother and the strangers around us, but the mood was too festive for fear. The VIP stand was decked in patriotic bunting. We were at a sanctioned observation point. Of course it was safe, they scoffed. Unconvinced, I decided how I would save myself.

When the music stopped, someone's wife smashed a bottle on the sub's bow and it shot out of the boat house like a cartoon banana from its peel. It hung in mid-air an instant before belly flopping like a breaching whale, raining droplets down on the crowd. Everyone clapped and cheered and screamed with delight. Everyone but me. I wrapped myself around a steel fence post and braced for the wave that was rolling toward us, three feet high and growing.

The crowd went silent, mesmerized by the swelling threat as the tidal wave surged closer. Then there were screams of astonishment and curses as everyone retreated in panic. The frigid water engulfed me to the waist and swept into the throng. Long tentacles of kelp tugged at my legs like a giant squid as I hugged the post. But this drenching, I knew, would be nothing compared to the backwash that must follow. People staggered to maintain their footing as the water rushed back into the river with a giant sucking sound. I rode it out on the fence's crossbar, proud of my foresight and miffed that no one had reached out for the kid on the brink.

It was the stuff of legend, but when the family compared notes thirty years later, we couldn't agree on even the most basic details.

"Summer? No, it was winter break," one brother insisted. "The weather was just unusually warm."

"The *Dolphin*? No, it was the *Spadefish*," the other brother corrected.

"It was the 660 boat, a Sturgeon class," my father said. "I forget the name, but it was the 660!"

"Band? I don't remember a band," said one of my tone-deaf brothers.

"You didn't get that wet. The water was only up to our knees," my mother said.

Her knees, maybe. The point is we couldn't agree because we were all right and wrong. It wasn't summer or winter break; it was Veteran's Day, which explains why we weren't in school. The date was November 11, 1969, one week before my tenth birthday, so technically I had my age wrong, too. It was 48 degrees that day—a little warm for

116

November, as one brother claimed, but far from summery. That meant I wasn't wearing my cut-offs as I remembered, but rather the pants that would become my favorite cut-offs the following summer. My father was right; it was the 660 boat— christened the *Sand Lance*, not the *Dolphin* or *Spadefish*. As for the boat's color, photographs prove it was black, not grey, and the nose was decorated with an enormous patriotic bull's eye of stars and stripes, a detail I can't imagine forgetting. Yet I did. News articles don't mention a band, and the photos don't show enough to prove whether or not there was one. Still, it completes the image for me and keeps the memory alive each time I hear "The Stars and Stripes Forever."

The sub was christened by the wife of Senator Thomas J. McIntyre, a three-term Democrat from New Hampshire, who was then in his second term. Five years later, I would campaign for his opponent with no recollection of McIntyre's name.

As I ponder that day, the most important detail to me now is the river. Piscataqua tugboat captains will neither confirm nor deny any ranking of the current's strength, but NOAA (National Oceanographic and Atmospheric Administration) lists it as one of the nation's strongest, in excess of four knots. The river is forty-four feet deep at Portsmouth Harbor where the shipyard is located, and November's water temperature averages forty-eight degrees. I shudder to think what could have happened if I were swept in.

As for the question of location, technically speaking, the Portsmouth Naval Shipyard is situated on Seavey Island in Kittery, Maine, but it borrows the name of the nearest city across the river in New Hampshire. Thus, each state claims it as their own.

It was a historic day, so I want to get it right. Someday my Maryland grandchildren will ask what's so special about that island with all the abandoned grey buildings—for abandoned it will most likely be by then, having already survived four decades of closure threats. I will want them to know how large the shipyard loomed in my life. Three generations of our family toiled there through five wars. The once mighty installation I saw from my bedroom window was illuminated at all hours of the night, a federal blight with a foot in each of my home states, the state where I was born and the state where I grew up, and I will not have my recollection become just another big fish story. These are the facts, as real as my sodden clothes.

# Downeast One-upmanship

Beth and I have been friends since high school, and simply put, she's brilliant. Has a PhD from Yale. Speaks half a dozen languages. Is comfortable with the literati or the computerati. And is urban to the core. I know she can't imagine my life here in Lubec and that she worries my brain cells aren't getting enough exercise. Beth travels a lot for her job, and she collects little things from exotic places to send me as gifts for Christmas and my birthday. These she wraps in the gift shop bags they came in, and packaging and gifts present me with linguistic and intellectual challenges. Like the small foil packets on which all of the writing was in another language and which could've contained either bath salts or food seasonings. I got suds when I added the contents to hot water so I guessed bath salts. But even with such testing, I'm sure I've got things from Beth in my bathroom cabinet that belong in my kitchen cabinet and vice versa.

This year for her birthday, I'm presenting Beth with a little challenge of my own. I bought her a present from West Quoddy Head Gift Shop, and I'm sending it in the bag on which is printed the conundrum: West Quoddy Head...Easternmost. I'll call Beth on her birthday and bide my time till she asks the question everyone always does: "How come it's called West Quoddy Head when it's the easternmost point in the US?" Then I'll answer with what I overheard one veteran volunteer at the Lighthouse explain: "Because we're on the west side of Grand Manan Channel, at the easternmost point in the US, at the end of South Lubec Road, in Lubec, Maine, the northernmost New England state." All four directions in one. That ought to leave Beth scratching her head for a bit.

—Susan Reilly

June bugs hurtle by.
Snub-nosed bullets in brown shells,
they'll knock your lights out.

—Danielle Woerner

## At the Supper Table

We eat roast moose (or is this caribou?)
sinewy in gravy, browsy still,
thick. Tastes like bark, like brush,
like that too slim distance
from the hunt.

So the telling hums and I've heard
all this before, the tracking, the cracked alders,
one animal with no place to run.
Sometimes a piece of shot gets caught
between my teeth. I extract it with a plink
into the porcelain plate.

> *Lined up the sights, braced myself.*
My mother sits up straight in her chair—
> *Don't go on like that, Hayward.*

—Carol Hobbs

## Cedar, Sage, Sweetgrass

Coyote and Raven laughed
as my claws got caught up
in the fine strands of sweetgrass
as I tried to braid

"Unh," I swore,
forgetting my human voice
I couldn't help myself
the smell of the earth
and sweetgrass brought out the claws

cedar, sage, sweetgrass

they found me in the
blueberry fields
outside of Calais
blue smacking lips
created a strange
contrapuntal line
to Raven's flight

Coyote stole from the edge
of the field looking cautiously

cedar, sage, sweetgrass

"Time for a trip"
"Unh, unh," smacked my lips

Coyote looked west,
stood on two legs
and tucked his hair

underneath his hat

cedar, sage, sweetgrass

"What of the medicine," I said
finding my voice

"We'll be back,"
said Raven flying away.

—Jason Grundstrom-Whitney

# Three Deer in Oquossoc

East will take me back. I drive
west. I wend between snowbanks,
until the road delivers me
to a sleeping boat launch.

They stand on the frozen ramp;
watch me with coats that are
better than mine. Ice houses
and snowmobiles edge the distance.

*I have to turn around*, I say
to them, *I went the wrong
way*. They stamp and chuff.
*No*, they tell me, *this is the way*.

—Sonja Johanson

# The Illuminati Owe Carl 57 Cents

## Rob Hunter

The day the Illuminati—secret, sinister—entered my life Harold Junior pulled up in his rusted-out Lincoln Continental as I was checking my mail. Our mailboxes, down by the road, do double duty as street addresses too, here in rural Maine. Harold's huge domestic battle cruiser had been bought cheap and came with a titanic appetite for gas and oil. But it never had to go far, only start. And it plowed through drifts that would stall a Jeep.

"Look. See that—it's a beaver." I followed Harold Junior's pointing finger. No beaver. There had been no beaver sightings on the lower Pennamaquan since they started blowing beaver dams to control upcountry flooding. Something about fish migrations.

Harold did not leave the driver's seat. This was a protocol of roadside conversations: stay in the car, otherwise they'll have to invite you inside for coffee or a beer. Anyway, Harold would have had a time making it to the house. His free spirit was sorely tried by arthritic knees and diabetes, trapped inside 450 pounds of fat.

"No, goddamn it, it's a beaver—*right there.*" Harold got out of the Lincoln. The car sprang eight inches up on its springs. They made those babies to last. Harold lurched toward the riverbank. The breeze caught the blue, syrupy exudations from his tailpipe and a cloud of hydrocarbons accompanied us as Harold grabbed my arm and dragged me along. He pointed. "There! A beaver."

"We don't see many of them," I said. I had never seen *any* of them.

Harold Junior released his hold on my arm. He grew thoughtful. "They renounce sex," he said. "The beaver bites its testicles off and throws them to the legions of hell in hot pursuit. A servant of God 'must cut off from himself all vices, all motions of lewdness, and must cast them in the Devil's face.' That was on TV." There was a Christian channel included in our local basic cable package.

"A pretty good reason for no beavers," I said. But beavers were making a comeback it appeared, and that is why I remember the day the Great White Lodge, The Illuminati, came to visit with me — Harold and the beaver. It was the same day and they came not bearing beavers, but with a wrong number.

It was Saturday about suppertime, the time boiler room calls come in. I have a routine, spooning rice and fish together, listening with courteous deference to the pitch, whatever, until the caller pauses for breath. Then I spring my trap. "My wife. You are calling for my wife. She died in April."

There is a pause and they ring off. Then I eat dinner. The University of Kansas Jayhawks are trying to build a new field house and the news of the death of a distinguished alumna has slowed them down but it hasn't stopped them. The Jayhawks' telephone solicitors still show up about once a month.

This time it was neither aluminum siding nor the Jayhawks.

I was watching *Talk Radio,* a video of a film from a stage play by Eric Bogosian, a film about the Faustian progression of a radio talk show host in Texas, most of it set in the broadcast studio. The phone rang. Hmmm.

I stopped the tape and answered the phone. A man in Windham, Maine was checking on a bogus charge on his bill. Had I received a call charged to his number? No. September fifth? I checked the calendar. I had been home all day waiting for chimney work. The caller later identified himself as Carl, a born-again Christian who listened to Christian radio stations. But all this information did not come at once; it was scattered throughout our conversation. We must have talked for ten minutes or so, he incurring charges far in excess of the $.57 he was checking up on. There had been a lot of billing mix-ups last month and he was calling all the listed numbers to frame a complaint. I was the first who had answered.

I said since the death of my wife I had lived alone with a

dog and two cats. Might they have learned to dial? No, besides this was a call to my number billed to his, from a third location.

Hmmm...

"Big Brother is here," said Carl.

"He's always been here," I replied, "except what with web-based media he'll be in our emails and movies, too." We grew easy and made observations about how computers were sending the world to hell.

"Next year. Two master numbers, supposedly known only to the National Security Agency and the National Science Foundation, and they can tap into your home CPU. We are at the mercy of any hacker."

Carl was easy to talk with, gregarious, out-going. And wary. Introductions were in order. "Hunter, Robert Hunter." Then gratuitously, "My kids use the same last name. But then, there wouldn't be any names on your bill." I could hear him nod and continued on into the silence. "They're almost thirty, not little kids who'd be playing telephone games." I held my hand in stages off the floor, indicating the heights of small children. He never gave me his last name even after I had told him mine several times, the repetitions in a context that my adult children had been visiting at about the time of his snaggled bill and perhaps one of their calling card calls to the coast had been misinterpreted by the NYNEX computer.

Carl brought up the Illuminati and the act of Congress that in 1913 created the Federal Reserve to keep foreign money manipulators out of our system. "But the secret control of the Federal Reserve. What about that? There is no way of finding out."

He had found out. Some Christian radio station had mentioned it. "I'll bet you see little hints in the news." I had told him I read news on the local radio station. Something I had been doing on one local radio station or another for almost forty years.

There were hints in the news, how would he know that? The wire services ground out reams of copy daily full of the gratuitous insights reporters slip in when they notice inconsistencies in the official versions of whatever the story of the day happens to be. Their editors flatten them out, seeing these as speed bumps on the unimpeded flow of homogenized information. During the news free-for-all of the Vietnam War, the daily press briefings in Saigon—the Five O'clock Follies generated a lot of these inconsistencies. Announcers learned to cherish them.

I was grinding out my penitent's path toward Social Security at a backwoods Maine radio station. Where I read the news. I was one of *them*. "A coffee grinder," a self-effacing reference to the limited wattage of the local radio station.

"There are hints. Can't deny it."

"Well, the Great White Lodge, right?" My first mistake; I thought I was playing Carl but launched into explanations of how these things came to be. My version the King James Authorized. My arguments sounded weak in the earpiece. "The Secret Masters are tying our shoelaces together while we sleep." There the ball was in Carl's court. I sensibly attributed the normalization of the news to a wire service self-censorship that kept the wackier stuff out of sight whenever an editor caught up with it. No one needed to know, the paper trails were too convoluted and too expensive to investigate.

"The Illuminati. It's Celtic." Keltic he said it, very PC: Celtic with a K. "Europe will take control of the North American money market, the world. A few control and direct everything, sharers of secret knowledge. There is a plan."

I was tempted to make a wisecrack but didn't. Enough worried people, feeling powerless, and they needed a target. Carl needed a target and he knew my number. Things were going to hell and God was on their side: the Christians needed a plan, a conspiratorial secret evil out there. Carl was thoughtful, not a crazy. These were things he had spent much time pondering. Not about plots, but about plots about plots. He had my number and my name while all I had was "Carl."

Carl explained, calming and confidential. This was something I, as a reasonable, educated human being knew, but for whatever reason, was not yet ready to face up to. He spoke a mumbo-jumbo of home brew mysticism, lifts from the rituals of lodges hopelessly garbled by centuries-long transmission."Illuminati, ever heard of 'em?" I had.The Illuminati, the behind-the-scenes master schemers of folklore and secret fears, had reentered my life. Carl was right: in his heart of hearts, everyone suspects that there are puppet masters controlling things. What else could explain so much misery if there is a just and merciful God?

Carl was worrying on about Europe taking over the world, so I didn't tell him I had seen a board game called "Illuminati" in the Dungeons and Dragons section of a science-fiction book store on a cobbled back street in Bonn, Germany just that April while taking a break from my late wife's last-ditch radiation treatments.

Carl was talking and I had not been listening. I hurried to catch up. "Illuminati, sure: pyramid power, Lovecraftian corruption, board room of the Chase Manhattan. Sure. Hey, ever read *Foucault's Pendulum*? Umberto Eco, you know?—*Name of the Rose*? They made a movie out of it."

Ahh, they made a movie out of it. Not to worry. There was an uncomfortable silence, just line noise and both of us breathing. Hollywood had executed a flanking maneuver, squeezed his fears onto the small screen, video to be compressed and downloaded. I decided Carl and I had talked enough. I would have just as happily agreed with him, but he would never allow it. He required contention and I was parroting a party line. He had gotten me to defending the established order. Anything I could say he could refute: the Rockefellers, the Rothschilds, tainted money impacted, ever circulating through the same hands, controlling.

"Goodbye, Carl."

"Goodbye, Robert."

I wished I had remembered to tell Carl not to worry, it's only a picture show.

And then there was the beaver.

# Privilege

Take, for example, the grass
in the suburbs of America,
how it forecloses the likes of
curly dock, tansy, clover,
creeping thyme,
buttercup, ragweed—
any raggedy brown
or blue or red or yellow
unruly thing
applying for entry here,
hoping to live and to flourish here—
all the so-called weeds,
all the beautiful wildflowers—
turned away, mowed down,
poisoned. And hasn't it always
been this way, only the pure,
cropped, decorous green
grass and its offspring welcomed here?
But at what cost to all of us
this skewed sense of beauty
and propriety, this monochrome
monoculture with its monotonous
traditions of separateness
and supremacy, totally lacking
in any flavor or utility
or spirit? The dispirited grass,
asleep in its vast bed
of privilege, dreams of the invading
hordes of color, riots
of dandelion, chicory, purslane,
which all make fine eating
and live on the other side,

out in the waste places,
out along the roadsides,
not very far away
but far enough away
so that the lonely, privileged,
uninflected grass begins to feel
a profound sense of loss,
a profound sense of sadness,
to think of the fine company
and the fine eating
of its despised neighbors,
all the brothers and sisters
whom it has never met
and does not know at all.

—Paul Hostovsky

# Falls Reversing

Black spruce is your red squirrel's first breakfast stop.
So that decision's been made. Still July hangs in the air,
a tern ready to pierce a tidal pool once a tidal pool appears.

They call the falls reversing, but it's more retrospective
than that. A portal that opens as it closes, as seals slide
and spout. I've got a pair of troubled gulls a man in a pickup

tells me. I got a morning slow as a row boat but bright as
a can of orange crush. Those aren't just waves crashing
against the shore, against a needle-colored grouse. Worlds mingle.

Words mingle. At the end of the marsh more marsh. Lost
in a forest of sticks, an abandoned whaler sinks into sea grass,
into what glaciers left behind as water and light flow together,

intertwined with time. Fog steps over stones too slippery
for most. Paddles fling up stars that dissolve before the next
strike is made. It's all in the tugging. The coast with its

currents, its reins. It pulls you in, even as it pushes you away.
Picnic tables plastered with pitch perch like crowns on
a cliff, above the tides that convince you stay, leave, stay.

—Susan Johnson

# Borrowed Dust

*Biddeford Pool, ME*

Praise be the fox who pauses
while I scout the marsh for the triller
whose song I don't recognize
and lays down to nurse her kit
on the warm blacktop curve.
Praise that which prevents
a car from rounding the curve
and the kit who after leaps
the old foundation and stays—
ears atwitch, brush tail and wheat tinted tip—
praise staying, stillness and looking—
to study me—as I study back. For shelters
they make for vixen and pup, praise shrub pine,
thistle, wild rose, honeysuckle, bearberry
that blanket the dunes—beach grass blown
like wild hair by the passed storm—praise
the storm that roils the bay, floods the cellar,
opens a leak in the roof—and the leak
its drip drip reminding me that the outside
wants to come in, as it did sometime
when the crumbling foundation was a house
west side overlooking the bay, marsh to the east—
praise the once home and its children,
pails, shovels, sand castles constructed
and their Persian domes, alligator molded
with razor clam shell teeth and the sculpted
woman, especially praise her pebble nipples.
Then praise the ocean—I do—that washed
them away, vines that crept
into the house, sun that dried

the wood and made it rot, termites,
their colonies and swarm intelligence
that ate it down. Praise what's left
of the stone foundation where
foxes hide and rest. Praise rest.

—Susan Nisenbaum Becker

# Eli-kisi-kikuhut Cihpolakon
## [EH-lee GHEE-zee GHEE-goo-hood JEEP-lah-g'n]
### (How the Eagle was Healed)


Fredda Paul


The eagle is ruler of the skies. When an eagle flies through all the birds have great respect and get out of the way. It's almost like putting down a red carpet.

It was a beautiful morning in late August, clear skies with a cool breeze coming off the ocean. Except there were no birds to be seen; even the seagulls weren't coming around. Everything had come to a standstill. It was as if all the winged creatures were already grieving over what would happen.

The sound of an eagle crying for help came to me like a premonition. I heard the cries all the way from Carlow Island up to the hill where I live. It sent cold chills through my body.

I grabbed a white bed sheet and caught a ride down to the beach. It was a bald eagle. When I found her, she was wedged between some big rocks at the edge of the shoreline screeching and flapping her good wing trying to fly away. She had been wounded by a gunshot. The tide had gone out, so she wasn't in immediate danger of being drowned. I knelt down and prayed to the Creator for the eagle to live. When I got close, I put tobacco on her injured wing and wrapped her in the sheet. I used the corner of the sheet to wrap her sharp talons so she wouldn't grab hold of me, then carried her to the road. I could tell she was female – they are larger than males and she was a heavy eagle. When I held her against my chest, I felt her heart against my heart; it was beating kind of fast because she was stressed out from being shot. I felt she was about to go into the next world, but when I held her she calmed down. That gave her good vibes that she was going to be well taken care of. My heart and her heart clasped together and her heart-beat evened out. I came to the eagle that day to be a part of her life. She was for me to heal.

When I got to the road, two guys gave me a ride in the back of their pick-up. When they asked, "What you got now, Fredda?" I just told them it was a wounded animal.

At the house, I left her wrapped in the sheet. This way, she wouldn't be so frightened. I put her on the floor in the medicine room and opened the top of the sheet to expose her head, then blew red willow smoke over her. That calmed her down and she never even screeched. Now I had enough time to make a cedar perch, but I came in the house every now and then to check on her and blow more red willow smoke to keep her calm. I already had ten 8-foot cedar logs I had cut and carried in from the woods, waiting to be taken to the sawmill so I could build an outhouse. I made the perch four feet off the floor – this way she would be high enough to look around, but not so high she couldn't get back up with the use of her one good wing.

The eagle's wing span was about eight feet, that's big for my small room. I put the perch diagonally so when she spread her good wing she wouldn't hit the medicine cabinet and other things. I used a welder's glove and helped her step on my arm to get onto the perch and secured one of her legs to the cedar with a five-foot piece of leath-er. Her tie allowed her to hop down on the floor, but not fly around and get hurt.

Now that she was calmed down, it was time to treat the wound. The bullet had gone right through and broken a bone on the elbow section of her wing. I used a poultice made of paqolus [BAH-gw'-looz] roots and boneset leaves to help heal the wound. These killed the pain and helped her bone start healing. I used red willow smoke again while I bound her injured wing to her body, almost like a splint, so she couldn't use it and crack the bone again. That was the first time she screeched after I brought her in the house. It was very piercing and hurt my ears to hear it; she was in excruciating pain. When I first blew red willow smoke in her face she shook her head back and forth like when a dog gets soaking wet they shake the water off, but it calmed her down.

Every couple days, I took the bindings off and applied fresh medicine, then gently wrapped her wing again. The first few times I did this, she tried to bite me, so I used the welder's glove. Later on, she seemed to understand what was going on. Then I could handle her bare-handed.

After two days, she calmed down enough to eat. I kept talking to her, and using red willow smoke and she gradually started to get used to me. At first I left her food on the floor, and she eventually got the courage to hop down and eat. Later on, she was taking mackerel from my hand. I fed the eagle fresh mackerel or salmon every day. During the spring and fall, as the tide was going down, salmon would swim up against the current through Passamaquoddy Bay into Gleason's Cove. At low tide, we would find a whole bunch of them in a deep hole over there, and throw in a net to bring them in. If I missed the tide, then people would give me fish.

At first, she ate two or three mackerel a day. A whole salmon might last her a couple days. She'd eat the belly of the fish first and carefully pick the meat off the rest until the bones were clean. When her appetite got better, she was going after seconds, thirds and fourths. She got kind of greedy later on, and even ate the bear and moose meat which I thawed out from my freezer.

Every time I went in the medicine room to be with the eagle I felt heartwarming chills. It was like I felt the spirit of the eagle entering my spirit. I named her "Fredda." I couldn't think of any female names for birds, and I always wanted to be an eagle. Only certain people knew I had an eagle in my house. I made sure all the blinds were drawn. When I asked the neighbors for newspapers to put on the floor, I told them I needed to wrap dishes. When I asked for more and more newspapers, they said, "You sure must have a lot of dishes, Fredda." She screeched when I played rock and roll on the radio; it wasn't piercing, just a small screech like she was telling me to cut down on the noise. I tuned to every station until I felt the eagle liked the music. She liked soft music, like a symphony orchestra. She would screech when

I ran the vacuum cleaner, so I used a broom instead.

After a few weeks, an elder came up to the house; she had a special way with birds and any kind of wild animal. She was a small woman and always dressed completely in black. She was a motewolon [m'-DEH-w'-l'n] (a person with extraordinary spiritual powers) and had a premonition that she could help the eagle. When the elder came in the medicine room, the eagle had positive feelings, she was very calm and they looked at each other eye to eye. The elder had the idea to make the eagle a hood to help calm her down. It would soon be time to take the wrappings off, but the eagle needed to stay for awhile longer. The elder went home and made the hood and came back the next day. The hood was made out of soft deerskin with an opening so the eagle could see out the front, but not side to side like eagles do. The elder smudged the hood and smudged the eagle. When she put it on, it was like putting a soft hat on a baby, that's how calm the eagle was. The elder tied the soft deerskin straps loosely around the eagle's neck, so if she shook her head it wouldn't come off. The deerskin hood stayed on the eagle until the day I let her go.

A couple weeks after the elder brought the hood for the eagle, I took the wrappings off and began exercising her injured wing. I gently moved the wing up and down a little at a time. If it hurt, she'd screech, not a loud one, just enough to say, "Hey, back off or else!" I kept exercising her wing morning and evening, and gradually she got used to it. Altogether, it took about three months for her to heal. One morning I went in the medicine room and she flapped her wounded wing. She did it twice, almost as if to tell me she was healing. After I exercised her wing, she flapped it four times. That is when I knew it was time to let her go. I didn't want to release her too early, but now I knew she was ready.

When the day came to let her go, I put a loose tie of red yarn around her left leg so if she came back I would recognize her. Then I wrapped her in a sheet to keep her calm. The ride I had arranged picked us up, then we stopped by and picked up the elder and headed back down to Carlow Island. I used the welder's glove to let her perch on my arm. The elder smudged the eagle and removed the deerskin hood. The eagle calmly looked around, then I pulled my arm way back and then swung forward with all my strength. When you do that, the eagle has to look up. She started out pretty good, but it looked like she was going to nosedive. She dipped down just a little, then flapped her wings and rose up to the sky and landed on the top branch of the tallest spruce tree around. From there, she could get a good take off. While she was up there she started exercising her wings to make sure the injured wing was doing its job. Then she spread her enormous wings and began her flight. She circled above my head a few times, then flew like an airplane across the ocean to Canada. I thought that was the last time I would see her.

When I got home, she was on the roof of my house. If only I had thought to take a picture, but I went to my freezer and got some fish instead. I threw a couple mackerel up to her and she caught them in her beak. She took off with a mackerel in each talon.

About a month later, the eagle came back. She had her mate with her, and they circled over my house, so close I could feel the wind off their wings. The red yarn I had wrapped around her leg was still there. It sent positive chills from my feet all the way to my head.

Eagles are very spiritual to our people. They send us the spirit of their body and soul. Friendships we have with eagles go way beyond the universe and tell us more than any human. They take us on a flight to places we have never been before.

She is always with me in spirit. There are days I see an eagle flying and know it is her.

# Turtle Island Turtle Rattle

Sarah Xerar Murphy

I will still be holding my father's turtle rattle when Bruce comes over to me after the ceremony that June of 2001, or that at least is how I remember his first speaking to me of her, I know this Mexican he'll say, this Mexican, though I doubt he will ask me then to adjust my route to take her with me across the first small piece of the continent I will have to negotiate on the long road back toward the Rockies, or mention how the trip would also include her boyfriend, though he will know enough about me to mention 1968. What I will be thinking about then is my father, and the memorial we have just put together at the Weald Bethel outside Cherryfield, and how we have stood in a circle and I have called in the directions each one represented by a hand carved decoy from his much loved collection, the beautiful oversized open mouthed calling loon he loved so much in its centre, doing my best to put together an indigenous ceremony that would celebrate his Choctaw heritage and the first peoples of the area after consultation with a Passamoquoddy spiritual leader fairer than I am. So that even after the circle has broken apart I will stand with my arms out to my sides and my hands open, my mind still flooded with memories of my conversations with my father over the years as if they still pour in from the directions I have called so that as Bruce speaks to me I think not of the young woman he is describing but of a call my father made to me way back in the eighties when I saw him little because I will already be out in Western Canada and he in Maine, my children young and travel expensive so we would meet most often back in Brooklyn and go sometimes for drinks in the bar where he met my mother, Montero's Bar and Grill, a Seaman's bar owned by a Gallego couple the New York Times says is the only dive bar left in Brooklyn as of this writing, home to hipsters though still with sailor made memorabilia on the walls and in cabinets perhaps even one of the model ships made from a turkey breastbone by my dad, the place he would hang out with my mom or other sailors while my brother and I ate paella in the back with the owners' kids, and too he would occasionally speak with the owners in the Spanish so different from theirs he had learned living with Yaki cousins along the Mexican border as an adolescent before he zoot-suited then joined the Navy underage to become a Pathfinder on Saipan before his eighteenth birthday.

And I will think of that Spanish, his fluency and his reading and his interest in the history of Indigenous America, the relationship between our Mississippian ancestors and Mesoamerica and how it drove me to Mexico to study pre-Columbian art and to stay there for at least five years longer than it took me to become completely bilingual, so that I was there in 1968. While it will be our mutual fluency that carries me back to the eighties as Bruce speaks to me, because those were the days long after I had moved from Mexico to Canada when I will be the principal Spanish interpreter for the Calgary courts and for Immigration Canada when the second great influx of refugees from Latin America occurs, not from the South American dirty wars and coups of the Kissinger dominated seventies but Central America that time, Salvadorans and Guatemalans from the Reagan backed civil wars and genocide of the eighties, when there will be morning after morning in the hearing room as individual testimony creates the archive of a country, torture techniques and murder methods cross-referenced to build believability, dark humour dominating the moments after, the immigration official who will turn to ask me and his fellow officer if we believed the testimony of a young man accosted by paramilitaries outside a restaurant, then as we nod say, Well somebody certainly shot him, and remembering the three scars far too close to the young man's liver place his fingers in a triangle in front of him to add, And a good shot too, did you get a look at the grouping?

Times when even I knew which way you had to walk to get around the border between Sweet Grass, Montana and Coutts, Alberta and though I never will tell anybody to do it I'll get home late one

Sunday night after a weekend in the mountains and find the repeated buzzing of hang-up after hang-up no message left on my answering machine and think to myself, something's happening I know something's happening, that it must be a Central American calling, Salvadoran, Guatemalan, someone still close to a life in the shadows a daily habit of resistance that will make the most important messages the least likely to be left, then find out that three friends of a good friend had arrived the night before after months of a troubled passage, moving up through Mexico and across the US border with more than twenty others in the false bottom of a van, their passports already burned before the crossing so that deportation would only be to Mexico if they were caught, then work in California and a slow undocumented passage north and that walk across their last border and their in-country asylum claim, affirming the question I can still recite in two languages that designates the five conditions that will find you to be a UN convention refugee, Do you have a well-founded fear of persecution on the basis of race, religion, nationality, social group or political opinion? giving being found a completely different meaning than it has in "Amazing Grace," but one easily as significant to the person who gets to say it.

While myself I'll be found without a job after helping them get found to be refugees because as far as Immigration is concerned I will have become too close to the community, something a little like colonial accusations of going native, and will ever after only sit in the hearing room to check the translations of others for Amnesty International. Which may be what I'll be doing as well as teaching English to adult immigrants by that time in the eighties my father calls me from Maine, the one I'll be thinking about standing outside the Weald Bethel still shaking his turtle rattle lightly in my hand to hear its sound, that time he asks me to talk to Délmi, a young Salvadoran woman on her way north to sanctuary and family in Montréal, because he'll be the only Spanish speaker in all of Cherryfield and environs and it would be nice for her to hear a woman's voice speaking her language. So that it will seem so ironically different by the time I focus on what Bruce is saying after we've sent my father off, our thoughts and prayers rising with the sweetgrass smoke while he speaks to me of that young Mexican woman in Cherryfield to rake blueberries, whose mother, like me, was active in 1968. And who surely does not need another Spanish speaker to talk to, but herself speaks for others on the barrens, with blueberrying so much changed since that conversation with my dad in the eighties. The Mi'kmaq from Canada will no longer be coming down to rake the blueberries, Latinos mostly from Mexico and Central America will be coming up, so that by the time I stand there turtle rattle in hand a Latino community will already be well established, and I don't know it yet but further along when I move back across Canada to New Brunswick almost ten years after that, I will be buying all my Mexican foods across the border in Maine, and there will be authentic taquerías to compete with Taco Bell, though I will know what everybody else who thinks about it knows, that once you invite people in to do your work for you, no matter the conditions, somebody stays, and that somebody plays welcoming committee to the next somebody and a community very quickly becomes inevitable, while in New Brunswick where there is a shortage of work most Latinos snuck across the border during that first wave of the Sanctuary movement have moved on into the larger Latino communities of Montréal, Toronto, Calgary, and Vancouver, though there is a wonderful Guatemalan restaurant in Saint John organized as a workers' co-op that doesn't use corn tortillas, New Brunswickers have not developed a taste for them they tell me, so I am still stuck leaving the country to buy mine, fresh when I can from Vázquez in Millbridge.

While of course, as I walk away from the broken circle to my father's refurbished brilliant green 1946 Dodge pickup that summer following his springtime death, its bed filled with flowers, pansies to bed out and the roses we will be setting out on the Narraguagus River along with his ashes on the outgoing tide, I will tell his old friend Bruce that I will be delighted to meet a young Mexican whose mother participated in the student movement of 1968, a turning point in Mexican history, though it will turn out that both she and I missed the Massacre in Tlatelolco which ended it, me by two days because I had been in New York at an international student conference and was invited to stay on to speak about the movement, she, her daughter tells me, because she was organizing in Mexico's north where this young woman was born. And by the time on the edge of fall as I prepare to leave I am asked to give her a ride I will know she is a university

142

student, that her mother's participation in the northwestern guerrilla movements in the seventies did not impede her, perhaps even helped her, to make sure her daughter got an education, and that the young woman's more southern Mexican boyfriend is a young man from the same university, his looks so much more mestizo than hers, typical really of the difference between the north of Mexico and its interior where so many more Indigenous survived the wars of conquest and the plagues, with the many Indigenous Mexicans you see in the border towns now, speakers of Zapotec, Mixtec, Nahuatl, and Maya are often enough internal refugees displaced by poverty from the heavily Indigenous states of Oaxaca, Guerrero, and Chiapas, and both of these youngsters raking berries not to support a family but on the migrant trail to earn money for a trip to Europe before returning to school, as many a young native Mainer too has done, which is why they both will find themselves able as most more pressured migrants will not, to confront the racism on the barrens when they find it, and speak out often for the others.

So that we will have that one night together in my camper when they will tell me of that as well as of their interest in the movements of *El Norte*, not only back in the sixties when I organized against the Vietnam War for the SDS but in the movements still going on around us, so that I will be dropping the young man off in New Hampshire to volunteer at the headquarters of The Bread and Puppet Theater, still going strong late in that summer of 2001, when we will sit talking and drinking the tequila one or the other of us has brought, before we disassemble the camper table for the young man to sleep while the young woman and I do the double bed above the truck cab, and I don't remember when it was in there that she got out her forged green card and she showed it to me laughing. But I will dream that night of travellers and adventurers and guerrilla fighters, of exiles and of refugees, and I will see them first in my father's people, in our Mississippi valley ancestors, removed from their farmsteads to make room for white farmers and the spread of slavery, an Indigenous diaspora seldom talked of in those terms even if they too were forced from their holy lands, their spiritual centres, with that word removal, Indian removal used instead, as if the people were a stain being blotted out, as if it were not an expulsion into exile like the expulsion too of the Jews and Muslims from Spain and other parts of Europe, and similar too in how as with any expulsion that does not achieve extermination, there will be those who stay and invite others back, a community re-forming, as in the Eastern Bands of Cherokee, Choctaw, and Creek, and in established Latino communities around the United States that continuously re-form even when attempts are made not only to expel those without documents but to burn down court houses to destroy the documents of those farmers whose land and citizenship and language rights were promised to them in the Treaty of Guadalupe Hidalgo, a treaty as violated as the treaties with indigenous peoples. And I will think of Délmi again and of others my dad took in over the years, and wonder whether, even in the work I have chosen for myself, there is something bred too in the bone of exile, in the transgenerational trauma of that euphemistically named removal that killed one fourth of those removed, that is more than just the ethics of an indigenous culture that bases its pride and its dignity in generosity rather than greed, in giving rather than possessing, that calls out for action in protection of the stranger, of the refugee.

Thoughts I will continue as I wake up somewhere still in Maine the next morning, pondering a continent so much in movement whether brutally forced or delight filled, the trails of tears and of joy, of a promised land and a land of broken promises as I ask myself perhaps for the first time how it is we make our Anglo distinction between Mexicans and Mexican Americans because all Mexicans are of course by definition Americans, deeply rooted children of this northern continent we have no other name for but that of an Italian explorer. Then when I leave both of these American Mexicans off one after the other, I will proceed on to Lake Champlain named too for yet another exploring European, the one who too founded the ill-fated colony on the island in the middle of the Saint Croix River on the border of what are now two countries, an island that I will pass once I make my move back east each time I drive to Saint Stephen to cross that border at Calais, while that evening by Champlain's lake whose native name I do not know, I will once more take out my dad's turtle rattle and with it call in the

144

directions to which we have scattered and I will move into a twi-light reverie imagining movement across this continent again, but this time from long before European arrival, and I will dazzle my-self with the kaleidoscopic variety of its languages and its peoples, of the Maya and maybe even Aztec traders, the *pochteca* who must have come to the towns and cities of my ancestors to meet them, the fluidity of the boundaries of this land's cultures and its lifestyles, how America, all of America, was a melting pot before it had that name or its impoverished European immigrants, persecuted and persecutor alike, a pot to piss in, nor the survival skills in the north to pass a winter or in more southern climes the knowledge to har-vest cacao or cochineal.

And I will think too of my dad and his leaving landlocked Oklahoma to sail the seven seas and all the other seas that have been added to that number since humanity learned to sail through-out the world, so that I might have asked myself too out of sheer fun if early Americans sailed west to Europe before Europeans came here, though I will have no idea that there is evidence a cou-ple from the Americas met Columbus in Galway in the 1480s, or that soon I will be in England again to notice how in Whitby as I am sure in other seaside towns the church has pews that say For Strangers, not to isolate but to give the stranger a place of welcome, I will think only of how my father will at last be welcomed home to a place he had never known, the Downeast Maine that combined the small country house of his boyhood dreams and the sea breez-es of his adult voyaging, and I will murmur to myself that refrain from my childhood, Home is the sailor home from the sea, and I will think again of how only the day before I had left the house he designed himself but never finished that has since become a gallery that bears his name, and how I had slept in the bed of his beautiful-ly rebuilt pickup among his collections of shotguns and of decoys and imagined him at twelve in Oklahoma earning a living on the reservation hunting and selling the ducks he brought down with neither decoys nor shotguns but with a single shot .22. And I will note how I too have already fallen in love with this country and with its native presence so that I already know I will keep coming back and back and back until I will finally move permanently to this downeast coast even as I choose to live on the other side of its artificial border.

And too there will be how I have just packed my own far less beautiful but more functional modern Dodge diesel pickup with the camper in its bed and placed in it the outsize calling loon last, sheltering it among the seat cushions so that first morning on the road it will greet me by the door where I have put it when we made the seats into a bed, while this second morning I will see only its head sticking up from the blankets as I go outside to sit at the picnic table of my campsite and hear living loons calling from the water, and I will get up to welcome the directions by that early dawn light then drive straight north alone to cross the border into Canada and once on the other side make my left turn to start the rest of the week long trip across the continent into Blackfoot territory, the Blackfoot presence still felt as the prairie meets the foothills, and I will arrive back home on September 8th, 2001 in time to receive a call from my mother three days later that I will almost miss because it is not yet seven-thirty in my time zone and she will tell me how her friend Olga Bloom at Bargemusic under the Brooklyn Bridge was doing yoga on her barge's deck and found herself watching as American Airlines Flight 11 crashed into the North Tower of the World Trade Centre so that I will already be on the phone before all the lines into New York jam up and hear in real time behind my mother's voice the falling of the Towers as she speaks to me from right across the river in Brooklyn, and I will know in the utter horror of that faraway sound that all of our ever more closely interconnected world, and in it this continent which I have spent the days of my drive imagining bounteous and boundaryless, has taken a xenophobic and fearful turn that means neither I nor anyone else will again cross at an official post without documentation that border I crossed eight times only weeks before with a simple Hello, How are you and Where are you going.

While over the years of living back on this coast I will continue to buy my corn tortillas in Maine and there will come a moment on the Deer Island-Campobello ferry when with great enthusiasm and in Spanish I will recommend the tacos at Vásquez as the best north of Mexico City to a Honduran getting ready to drive down the coast, and I will lean up against his car to draw him a map as to how to get there, and maybe there will be something in the enthusiasm and length of our exchange that makes someone think they have seen something and they have to say something, but I will be stopped and searched for the first time in years when I get to that easiest of border crossings between Campobello and Lubec, and while they do not take my truck apart I will have to take out the few meds I always carry and explain what they are and point out that my Advil liquigels are indeed Advil, even if they are not in the package they came in the word itself is stamped in white on the side of each bright green capsule. And once home again I will remember that young woman laughing in my camper and showing me her forged green documentation as we drank that last night in Maine in the last days of that long ago summer that will eventually bring me east and I will wonder if she has kept up the social justice work that interested her so much back then, and if she does it here or in Mexico, in the United States or in some other country, and I will think how people move like water and water always finds a way, no matter the slow dripping or sand sharp grinding cost of it, and I will take out my father's turtle rattle and think not just of his clan, how he was Turtle clan of the Choctaw Nation, but of Turtle Island, and of how in our many nations we are all her children.

And it is then I will run my hands over the rings of the turtle's back and shake the rattle again and think of the pews in Whitby and I will breathe deep and the image of the body of a small Syrian boy picked up on a beach, a boy whose relatives in Canada wanted him to come home to them, will spring into my mind and be followed by Africans crossing the Atlantic, not in the Middle Passage but still to America, South and Central, to make their way north crossing borders in conditions as difficult and sometimes as crowded as any slave ship, the circumstances of their travel its own form of extreme vetting, and too of the Central Americans themselves coming northward endangered now by the gangs formed originally from the paramilitaries active in the civil wars, and how it is this winter of 2017 that once more that stream of refugees, yet another new underground railroad, has its terminus in Canada. And then there will come times I'll stand on the Canadian side of the St. Croix River looking across the border wondering how and where and when the in-country claims are being made and how many people it is right now and in what language are reciting that question central to the UN convention on refugees: Do you have a well-founded fear of persecution on the basis of race, religion, nationality, social group or political opinion? And I will ask myself how many will be stopped before crossing, how many die on the way, how many lose fingers and toes to frostbite out west before the floods come—and how many will be found. And I will think of my father and of Délmi and I will burn sweetgrass and call the directions and remember my Guatemalan friends in the false bottom of that van and continue to ponder: If we cannot find a way to welcome and treat fairly with the stranger, how we will ever find our own way home.

# Contributors

**Michael Brown** began teaching in 1962, and he began writing then. He has had four books of poetry published, and numerous other articles, essays, and pieces of journalism. Right now, he is College Transitions Instructor at Axiom where he is helping young people earn their high school credentials. He also helps older writers get their books and articles published. He and his partner live in Downeast Maine where they have a lovely estate and take in retired sled dogs.

**Dennis Camire** currently teaches college writing and creative writing at Central Maine Community College and at White Mountains College. Additionally, he's on the board of Maine Poetry Central which curates The Portland Poet Laureate Project and the poetry series, In Verse: Maine Places and People, which appears in The Sun Journal Sunday Edition. His last book, *Stone By Stone: Poems about the Art of Dry Stone Walling*, was published by Finishing Line Press. He lives in an A-frame in West Paris, Maine.

**Wendy Cannella** lives in York Harbor, near Brave Boat Harbor, less than a mile to Harbor Beach and a walk through the woods to Long Sands in southern Maine. I am so grateful to call this wonderful state my home, with all of its wonderful heritages, and to continue to be so lucky as to look out over the rocks at our blue-grey horizon.

**Barbara Chatterton**: It's exciting to share one of my early experiences in Downeast Maine, to revisit those days when everything was fresh and strange and full of mysterious promise. This part of Maine is my adopted home. As with any kind of family, I had to range far & wide before I realized how completely I belong to it, and it belongs to me. To live elsewhere is unthinkable. When I'm not writing, you can find me with my family and friends, tending my farm, and tilting at windmills.**Dan**

**Crowfeather McIsaac** was born into mainstream society 60 years ago, but has been walking the 'Red Road' since meeting his late wife Muin'iskw in 1999. Before that, he had no firm beliefs, except there was some guiding hand behind the universe. He could not accept the teachings of Christianity, because there seemed to be too many layers between himself and Creator. Daniel respects the spiritual choices of anyone who is sincere in their beliefs, and who does not use their religion to harm others. When he learned the teachings of traditional Mi'kmaw spirituality from Muin'iskw, they spoke to the Cree blood he carries—he had found his way at last.

**Frances Drabick** lives in Eastport, Maine where she reaches out to the world through poetry and short stories on her website: FrancesDrabick-WritesIt.com. Drabick has been awarded two nominations for the Pushcart Prize in poetry, and has been published in various periodicals.

**J. C. Elkin** is an optimist, linguist, singer and M.F.A. candidate at Bennington Writing Seminars. I am the author of *World Class: Poems Inspired by the ESL Classroom* and other works drawing on spirituality, feminism, travel, and childhood appearing domestically and abroad in such journals as *The Delmarva Review, Kestrel*, and *Angle*. I was born in Maine, spent my summers there, and graduated from Bates College before leaving New England in the Eighties. My father still lives in Kittery. For more information, please visit my website, www.jcelkin.net

**Kathleen Ellis**: "In Lubec in the late 1970s, I was constantly aware of living on the edge of the country, but I was made especially aware of the close concerns and activities between the U.S. and Canada due to my in-laws' memories of Eleanor Roosevelt's crossings by ferry from Lubec to Campobello." A recipient of poetry fellowships from the National Endowment for the Arts and Maine Arts Commission, Ellis has taught English and Honors at the University of Maine in Orono since 1992. Poems from her manuscript, "Dear Darwin," were set to music and released as a Parma Recordings CD, which was nominated for a 2015 Grammy Award. Ellis coordinates the annual POETS/SPEAK! fest at the Bangor Public Library and teaches summer poetry workshops at the Farnsworth Art Museum in Rockland.

**Jéanpaul Ferro** is a novelist, short fiction author, and poet from Scituate, Rhode Island. A 10-time Pushcart Prize nominee, his work has appeared on National Public Radio, Contemporary American Voices, Columbia Review, Salzburg Review, and others. He is the author of *Essendo Morti – Being Dead* (Goldfish Press, 2009), nominated for the 2010 Griffin Prize in Poetry; and *Jazz* (Honest Publishing, 2011), nominated for both the 2012 Kingsley Tufts Poetry Prize and the 2012 Griffin Prize in Poetry. He is represented by the Jennifer Lyons Literary Agency. Website: www.jeanpaul-ferro.com

**Stephanie S. Gough** is a creative non-fiction writer from Campobello Island, New Brunswick. She comes from a long line of pirates and smugglers, and currently holds three passports.

**Jason Grundstrom-Whitney** currently works at Riverview Psychiatric Center as a LADC/LSW. He is a writer, poet, and musician who has played in bands and read his poetry across America. Jason has mixed ancestry: Traditional Bear Clan member of the Passamaquoddy/Irish/Scottish/Welsh. The poems are taken from a working series: "Bear, Coyote, Raven."

**Grey Held** is a recipient of an NEA Fellowship in Creative Writing. Held has two books of poetry published, *Two-Star General* (Brick Road Poetry

Press in 2012) and *Spilled Milk* (Word Press in 2013). Held works closely with the Mayor's Office of Cultural Affairs in Newton, MA to direct projects that connect contemporary poets and their poetry with a wider audience. He is also a visual artist whose drawings have been exhibited in museums and galleries nationwide.

**Leonore Hildebrandt** is the author of *The Work at Hand* and *The Next Unknown*. A third collection, *Where You Happen to Be*, will be forthcoming in 2018 (Deerbrook Editions). She has published poems and translations in the *Cafe Review, Cerise Press, Cimarron Review, Denver Quarterly, Drunken Boat, The Fiddlehead*, and *Sugar House Review*, among other journals. Winner of the 2013 Gemini Poetry Contest, she received fellowships from the Elizabeth George Foundation, the Maine Community Foundation, and the Maine Arts Commission. She was nominated twice for a Pushcart Prize. A native of Germany, Leonore lives "off the grid" in Harrington, Maine. She teaches writing at the University of Maine and serves on the editorial board of the Beloit Poetry Journal.

**Andrea Suarez Hill** had a career in print, television, and photojournalism before moving to Jonesboro, Maine. She's inspired by nature and the wild life on her salt water farm which she and her husband, Arthur, share with their horses and pets. Her work has been published in *The Aurorean, Harvest Recess, Picker Shacks: A Living History of Northern and Downeast Maine*, and *The Horse's Maine and New Hampshire*.

**Carol Hobbs** is originally from Newfoundland, Canada and moved to Massachusetts in the mid-1990's following the collapse of the fishery, and in the mass migration of islanders to parts of mainland Canada and beyond. Her poems have appeared in *The Malahat Review, Fiddlehead, The Antigonish Review, Cider Press Review, Appalachian Heritage, Riddle Fence*, and other magazines, journals, and anthologies in Canada, Ireland, and the United States. Her book manuscript, *New Found Lande*, received a PEN New England Discovery Prize, and under its new title *The World's Last Polar Bear*, was named a semifinalist for the 2017 Perugia Press Prize.

**Paul Hostovsky** is the author of nine books of poetry, most recently *Is That What That Is* (FutureCycle Press, 2017). His poems have won a Pushcart Prize, two Best of the Net awards, and have been featured on Poetry Daily, Verse Daily, and The Writer's Almanac. He makes his living in the Boston area as an ASL interpreter and Braille instructor. Visit him at www.paul-hostovsky.com

**Rob Hunter** is the sole support of a large orange cat and the despair of his young wife. He does dishes, mows the lawn and keeps their coastal Maine cottage spotless by moving as little as possible. Rob's wife, Bonnie, is the secretary at a nearby rural elementary school; they live on America's northeastern border with the Canadian Maritime Provinces. Please note that the border is on the southwest if you are in Canada. This is important if you are not a swimmer.

**Cynthia Huntington**, a Maine native, grew up in a single parent home. Her mother cut and packed sardines for Trident Fish Factory. Her earliest memories consist of fog horns, tugboats and the cry of seagulls. Her mother's hands. Cynthia's stories are reflections of the people she has known and her own experiences combined with her own point of view and condensed into short stories.

**Sonja Johanson** has recent work appearing in the Best American Poetry blog, *BOAAT*, *Epiphany*, and *The Writer's Almanac*. She is a contributing editor at the *Eastern Iowa Review*, and the author of *Impossible Dovetail* (IDES, Silver Birch Press), *all those ragged scars* (Choose the Sword Press), and *Trees in Our Dooryards* (Redbird Chapbooks). Sonja divides her time between work in Massachusetts and her home in the mountains of western Maine. You can follow her work at www.sonjajohanson.net.

**Susan Johnson** lived in Nova Scotia, where her mother was born, for seven years before returning to New England. She teaches writing at UMass Amherst where she received her MFA and PhD. She has had poems published in *Poet Lore*, *Quarterly West*, *Poetry Northwest*, *Massachusetts Review*, and others. She lives in South Hadley, MA, where she eats a lot of kale.

**J. Kates** is a minor poet, a literary translator and the president and co-director of Zephyr Press. He has been awarded three National Endowment for the Arts Fellowships, an Individual Artist Fellowship from the New Hampshire State Council on the Arts, and the Cliff Becker Book Prize in Translation for the *Selected Poems of Mikhail Yeryomin* (White Pine Press, 2014). He has published three chapbooks of his own poems: *Mappemonde* (Oyster River Press), *Metes and Bounds* (Accents Publishing), and *The Old Testament* (Cold Hub Press) and a full book, *The Briar Patch* (Hobblebush Books). He is the translator of *The Score of the Game and An Offshoot of Sense* by Tatiana Shcherbina; *Say Thank You and Level with Us* by Mikhail Aizenberg; *When a Poet Sees a Chestnut Tree and Secret Wars* by Jean-Pierre Rosnay; *Corinthian Copper* by Regina Derieva; *Live by Fire* by Aleksey Porvin; *Thirty-nine Rooms*, by Nikolai Baitov; Genrikh Sapgir's *Psalmsand Muddy River*, a selection of poems by Sergey Stratanovsky. He is the translation editor of *Contemporary Russian Poetry*, and the editor of *In the Grip of Strange Thoughts: Russian Poetry in a New Era*. A former president of the American Literary Translators Association, he is also the co-translator of four books of Latin American poetry.

**Chuck Kniffen** co-owns and operates Turtle Dance Totems sea-junk studio and arts cooperative, with his wife, Rhonda Welcome, in Lubec, Maine. He is a combat wounded veteran of the Vietnam War who has been penning bits and pieces since his discharge from the Green Machine. Chuck finally finished a book length war/memoir, *Fifty Years in a Foxhole*. In his wealth of free time he is an all-season kayaker, paddling in circles over the North Atlantic singing praise to...well, he says its "singing praise" but you couldn't tell by asking the urchin divers what that unholy racket was.

Michele Leavitt, a poet and essayist, is also a high school dropout, hepatitis C survivor, and former trial attorney. Her essays have appeared in venues including *Guernica, Catapult,* and *The Journal. Poems* appear recently in *North American Review, concis, Gravel,* and *Baltimore Review.*

A native New Yorker, **Carl Little** has lived in Somesville since 1989. He holds degrees from Dartmouth, Middlebury and Columbia. Prior to joining the staff at the Maine Community Foundation in 2001 as director of communications and marketing, he directed the public affairs office and the Ethel Blum Gallery at College of the Atlantic. Little has published two collections of poetry: *10,000 Dreams Explained* (Nightshade Press) and *Ocean Drinker: New & Selected Poems* (Deerbrook Editions). His poems have appeared in a number of journals, including *Black Fly Review, Off the Coast, Hudson Review,* and *Maine Times,* as well as in several anthologies edited by Wesley McNair. His poetry was recently featured in the Maine Sunday Telegram's Deep Water series, edited by Gibson Fay-LeBlanc, and read by Stuart Kestenbaum in "Poems from Here" on Maine Public Radio.

**Joyce Joslin Lorenson** lives in Rhode Island, U.S.A., grew up on a dairy farm and records the daily happenings in nature around her rural home. She has been published in several print and electronic journals.

**Donna M. Loring** is an elder and present council member of the Penobscot Indian Nation. She held the position of the Nation's Representative to the Maine State Legislature for over a decade. She authored and sponsored LD 291 "An Act to Require Teaching Maine Native American History and Culture in Maine's Schools" which Governor Angus King signed into law on June 14th 2001. **The law is changing the way Maine views it's history.** Loring is a graduate of the University of Maine at Orono where she earned a Bachelor of Arts in Political Science. Donna is the President of Seven Eagles Media productions, a Vietnam Veteran (Long Binh 1967-1968), and author of *In the Shadow of the Eagle: A Tribal Representative in Maine,* a journal of her experiences in the Maine State Legislature as a Non-voting Tribal Representative. She the author of the musical *Glooskape Chronicles Creation* and the *Venetian Basket.* Donna was featured in the Maine Sunday Telegram as one of ten women "Making a Difference in Maine" and making Maine a better place to live and hosts a monthly radio show, "Wabanaki Windows" on WERU Community Radio. The University of New England houses her papers and sponsors an annual lecture series in her name. Donna is a member of the Deborah Morton Society of the University of New England and a member of the International Women's Forum (IWF). In 2017, Donna was awarded an honorary doctorate degree from the University of Maine.

**Frederick Lowe** is a half-time resident of Maine, a full-time poet, and a semi-retired psychotherapist. Lowe has had a home in the far Downeast for nearly 45 years, and the region has inspired most of his work. Fred "came back" to Maine, his paternal family having come from Deer Isle, ME to Brooklyn, NY more than 100 years ago, recruited as New York Harbor

Pilots. A great-great grandmother was a Penobscot Native American. Fred is a two-time Pushcart nominee and has published in a number of print and on-line journals in the US, Great Britain, and Ireland. See fredlowe-poet.com

**Sharon Mack** is a retired journalist living on the bold coast of Downeast Maine. After 35 years of telling other people's stories, she is now telling her own. She has been previously published in *Left Hook*, *The Feminine Collective*, *Working Waterfront* and *The Bangor Daily News*. She won the 2017 Prize in Prose Award from *five80split* literary and arts journal.

**Dr. Charles McGowan** is happy on either side of the northeast U.S./Canada border. He crossed it from birth in 1931 through the present and revived tales of farm, forest, friends, and family in a recently authored book. He had the good fortune to marry an artist who loved the coastline from Cape Cod to Calais as much as he appreciated the Great North Woods. They nurtured ten children while he practiced oral and maxillofacial surgery. A natural story-teller committed to heritage, he blends first hand with research when paying homage to each account, legend, or yarn.

Poet **Mark Melnicove** lives in Dresden and is a former publisher and editor. Melnicove received his MFA in literature and writing from Bennington College and teaches creative writing, humanities, and film studies at Falmouth HS, Falmouth, Maine. He is also a member of the faculty of the USM Stonecoast MFA in Creative Writing program and has been executive director of the Maine Writers and Publishers Alliance. He was one of the founders of Tilbury House Publishers in Gardiner, ME.

**Rowan Miller** is a 3rd year Creative Writing and Political Science student at University of New Brunswick Fredericton. He is also the 2014 winner of the Walter Edgar Prize in Youth Short Prose from the University of South Carolina Honours College, judged by the late Pat Conroy. Rowan is fascinated by the intersection of the hidden and cultures and histories that together form the mosaic of Canadian and American life. Though born in British Columbia, he spent many years in SC, and his family traditionally hails from the Maritimes, with a history that goes back hundreds of years on the Kingston peninsula. He is trying to get in touch with the Maritime experience, its isolation, history, and divisions through writing.

**Caroline Misner** is a graduate of Sheridan College of Applied Arts & Technology with a diploma in Media Arts Writing. Misner's poetry, fiction and non-fiction have appeared in journals throughout the USA, Canada, India, and the UK, as well as anthologies and webzines. She writes erotica under the pseudonym Cynthia Lucas and her stories have appeared in several publications and anthologies. In 2009, she was nominated for the prestigious Writers' Trust/McClelland & Stewart Journey Anthology Prize as well as a Pushcart Prize in 2010 and 2011.

**Sarah Xerar Murphy**: Interpreter, translator, community activist, award winning author; performance, visual and spoken word artist, Sarah Xerar Murphy has published, performed, shown, and toured in Mexico, Spain, the United States, United Kingdom, and Canada. Winner of Canada's Golden Beret Award as well as an Arts Council England International Artist's fellowship, Murphy has eight books and one sound art/spoken word CD to her credit. Of Choctaw, Irish, English, German, and Latino heritage, Murphy was encouraged from childhood by her Choctaw father, William D. Sherar to view our Turtle Island as one world. Brought up in Brooklyn, she has spent her adult life in Mexico and Canada, and currently in Bocabec, New Brunswick. Her work as a refugee advocate and worries about our world's turn toward xenophobia, as well as her love of her new home, are reflected in her piece.

**Susan Nisenbaum Becker's** poetry has appeared or is forthcoming in *The MacGuffin, Crab Orchard Review, Harvard Review, Salamander, Comstock Review, Slipstream, Calyx* and *Talking Writing* among others. She is a playwright, actor and arts organizer for which she has received numerous Local Massachusetts Cultural Council Grants, and has been a feature on local cable television arts programs. Susan has been awarded residencies at the Banff Center for the Arts, Yaddo, the MacDowell Colony, the Ragdale Foundation and the Virginia Center for the Creative Arts, and was nominated for a 2012 Pushcart Prize. Her first full-length book of poems, *Little Architects of Time and Space*, was published by WordTech Communications/ Word Poetry in 2013.

**Ellie O'Leary** writes about growing up in the village of Freedom, Maine. She has won the Martin Dibner Memorial Fellowship in poetry, is the previous host of Writers Forum on WERU-FM, and has taught at Pyramid Life Center (NY) and Belfast (Maine) Senior College. She has an MFA in poetry from the Stonecoast MFA program. www.EllieOLeary.com

**Fredda Paul**, is a Passamaquoddy elder and healer from the Pleasant Point reservation in Maine. One of the most influential people in Fredda's life was his grandmother, Grace Lewey. She was a well-respected medicine woman, and became Fredda's teacher and mentor from the time he was a teenager, upon his return from Indian Residential School in Nova Scotia. Because of his enthusiasm for learning, it wasn't long before he was chosen by his grandmother to carry on the tradition of Passamaquoddy medicine. His mother, Annie Paul, was a well-known sweet grass braider and a spiritual leader of the tribe. She raised eight children, working for many years in the sardine factory. She spoke mostly Passamaquoddy and enough of the English language to communicate very well. Fredda's father, Michael Paul, was Mik'maq – from Escasonie, Nova Scotia. In 2007, Fredda was given an honorary citation from Unity College for his work to keep traditional medicine alive.

**John Perrault** is the author of The Ballad of Louis Wagner (Peter Randall Publisher, 2009), Here Comes the Old Man Now (Oyster River Press, 2005), and Jefferson's Dream (Hobblebush Books, 2009.) His poetry has appeared in *Christian Science Monitor, Commonweal, Blue Unicorn, Off the Coast,* and elsewhere. He was Poet Laureate of Portsmouth, NH, 2003–2005. www.johnperrault.com

An Oregon native, **Patrick Gentry Pierce** has found his true home in the Northeast. A life-long practicing sculptor and poet, Pierce lives and works on his ArtFarm in Saco, Maine. He studied Literary arts at Trinity College and sharpened his wits in New York, with a further degree at Adelphi. He is active in the New England poetry circuit, and his latest book of poems, *Telegraphs,* will be published in this spring.

**Bruce Pratt** is the winner of the 2007 Ellipsis Prize in poetry and a finalist for the Erskine J. Poetry award from Smartish Pace. His poems have appeared in *The Book of Villanelles* from Knopf's Everyman Series, the anthology *Only Connect* (Cinnamon Press, Wales), *Smartish Pace, Puckerbrush Review, The Hiram Poetry Review, The Naugatuck Review,* and many similar publications in the United States and abroad. Pratt's poetry collection, *Boreal,* is available from Antrim House Books. Pratt edits *American Fiction* and is the past Director of the Northern Writes Project at Penobscot Theatre Company. He graduated from Franklin and Marshall College with a BA in Religious Studies, the University of Maine with an MA in English, and the University of Southern Maine's Stonecoast MFA in Creative Writing program with a degree in creative writing. He and his wife, Janet, live in Eddington, Maine. www.bepratt.com

**Patricia Smith Ranzoni**: Born up the Penobscot River in Lincoln, Maine in 1940 to a Canadian-American woodsman from Webster Plantation and an 8th generation Yankee farm girl of coastal Maine, both descended from mixed Native and European wilderness and border/borderless peoples as far back as can be found, so far, in what became Maritime Canada and Maine, Patricia Smith Ranzoni and family tend one of the subsistence farms of her youth in Bucksport, where her father became a rigger at the paper mill after WWII and where she has been named Poet Laureate "for as long as she shall live." A retired education and mental health consultant, she is self- and folk-schooled in poetry to which she turned in midlife to document the disappearing ways of her people. Published across the U.S. and abroad, her work is drawn from for courses and archives of Maine's writers and history and class, most recently in *Bedding Vows, Love Poems From Outback Maine* (North Country Press 2012), her twelfth title; and an anthology, *Still Mill, Poems, Stories & Songs of Making Paper in Bucksport, Maine* (North Country Press, 2017) of which she is editor.

**Susan Reilly** is the originator, editor, and publisher of *The Fridge: a Lubec Community Calendar. The Fridge* includes Ms. Reilly's short column "From the Back of The Fridge." Ms. Reilly is a former columnist for *Lights on Lubec, The Lubec Light,* the *Maine Women's Journal,* and the *Seguin Beacon.* The author has had essay published in the former *Maine Times* and aired on *Maine Public Radio.* Her work appeared in the *Aputamkon Review,* Volumes

1,2,3, and 4. Ms. Reilly's e-book, *Readers' Revenge: A Book Group Novel* is available online. The author lives year-round in Lubec.

**Bunny L. Richards** lives in a log cabin in Trescott Township which she built with her husband, Lew, in 1981. Her family in Trescott includes their cat Emmy Lou and resident porcupines, Baby G. and Margie. Bunny's passions are reading, writing, and listening to Red Sox baseball on the radio.

**JD Rule**, the Resident Novelist in the easternmost town in the United States, has ten titles currently in print, including eight novels. Most deal with that elusive boundary that separates people, even when they are unaware of the sharp edges. Rule earned his MBA before moving to Maine, and has never looked back. The son of a cold-war military officer who attended four high schools, he has lived on both coasts, abroad, in the heartland, and draws from experiences collected along the way. Much of his career involved the auto industry as a customer-relations manager charged with keeping owners happy and the company out of court, providing a rich background for fiction. Since arriving in Maine he has coached creative writing as an adjunct to a popular music education program, writes for the local newspaper, and currently has two new works in the hopper. His most treasured award is for perfect attendance at North Kingston Junior High, in Rhode Island.

**Cheryl Savageau**, of Abenaki and French Canadian heritage, was born in central Massachusetts. She graduated from Clark University in Worcester, Massachusetts, and studied writing at the People's Poets and Writers Workshop in Worcester. She is the author of the poetry collections *Home Country* (1992), *Dirt Road Home: Poems* (1995) nominated for the Pulitzer Prize, and *Mother/Land* (2006). Savageau's poetry retells Abenaki stories, often focusing on the unrecognized lives of women and the working class; her work is enriched by the landscape and ecology of New England. Her knowledge of lakes, ecology, and the importance of storytelling informed her children's book *Muskrat Will Be Swimming* (1996), a winner of the Notable Book for Children Award from the Smithsonian and the Skipping Stones Book Award for Exceptional Multicultural and Ecology and Nature Books. Savageau has received grants from the National Endowment for the Arts and the Massachusetts Arts Foundation. She has been a mentor to Native American writers through the Wordcraft Circle of Native Writers and Storytellers.

**Catherine Schmitt** is the author of *A Coastal Companion: A Year in the Gulf of Maine from Cape Cod to Canada*, *The President's Salmon: Restoring the King of Fish and its Home Waters*, **and** *Historic Acadia National Park*. Her writing has appeared in newspapers, magazines, and literary journals including *Island Journal*; *Maine Boats, Homes & Harbors*; *Friends of Acadia Journal*; *Terrain*; **and** *1966*. Schmitt has undergraduate and graduate degrees in environmental science, and has worked in lakes, streams, wetlands, and beaches throughout the Northeast. She earned a Stonecoast MFA in creative nonfiction in 2012. As communications director for Maine Sea Grant, Schmitt conveys research findings and information about ocean and coastal issues to various audiences. A Coastal Companion is part of this effort, as is her role as managing editor for The Catch: Writings from Downeast Maine. Catherine Schmitt is on the Maine Writers & Publishers Alliance Board of Directors, the Maine Atlantic Salmon Museum Board of Directors, and the Board of the Somes Pond Center. She is a member of the National Association of Science Writers.

**Lee Sharkey** is the author of *Walking Backwards* (Tupelo, 2016), *Calendars of Fire* (Tupelo, 2013), *A Darker, Sweeter String* (Off the Grid, 2008), and eight earlier full-length poetry collections and chapbooks. Her recognitions include the Ballymaloe International Poetry Prize, Abraham Sutzkever Centennial Translation Prize, the Maine Arts Commission's Fellowship in Literary Arts, the Maine Writers and Publishers Alliance's Distinguished Achievement Award, the RHINO Editor's Prize, the Shadowgraph Poetry Prize, and Zone 3's Rainmaker Award in Poetry. She teaches creative writing to adults recovering from mental illness and serves as senior editor of the Beloit Poetry Journal.

**Grace Sheridan** and her spouse Neil live in Cutler, Maine. Her life story includes Acton, MA, Gordon College, fourth grade classrooms, two sons, Civil Service, and a granddaughter. She credits Sunrise Senior College instructors and the Salt Coast Sages for encouraging her post-retirement interest in poetry.

**Karen Skolfield's** book, *Frost in the Low Areas* (Zone 3 Press), won the 2014 PEN New England Award in poetry. She is the winner of the 2016 Jeffrey E. Smith Editors' Prize in poetry from The Missouri Review and has received awards and fellowships from the Poetry Society of America, New England Public Radio, Massachusetts Cultural Council, Split This Rock, and elsewhere. She teaches writing to engineers at the University of Massachusetts.

**Karin Spitfire** is an artist whose chooses her medium to match her need for expression. Her major forms are poetry and artist books. Spitfire has studied writing with Barbara Maria and book arts at USM with Rebecca Goodale, at Haystack and Pendland with Eileen Wallace. She currently runs a letterpress studio at the Steelhouse in Rockland with graphic designer Richard Smith. Spitfire is the author of *Standing with Trees* and *Wild Caught*. Her poetry has been published in numerous print and on-line literary magazines, and she was Poet Laureate of Belfast, Maine in 2007 & 2008.

**Elizabeth Sprague** earned her MFA in Creative Writing at Mills College with a collection of short stories and was twice awarded the Reinhardt Prize for Fiction. She has been Co-Director of the Bay Area Writers' Workshop and a reader at *Fish Stories,* a literary journal, in Chicago. Elizabeth is listed in *Feminists Who Changed America 1963-1975.* She lives in East Machias and teaches fiction writing in the Amherst Writers & Artists Method. Her short fiction has been published in *The Walrus* and *Bakunin. This That*

*This* has been featured in The Equinox Petroglyph Exhibition, a multimedia response by Indigenous and European-descent women and children to the petroglyphs of Machias Bay.

**Emma Suárez-Báez** holds a Master's Degree in Bilingual Education and works with children and teachers at P.S. 340 in Bronx, New York. She left Puerto Rico at seventeen to pursue a career as a professional dancer in New York City. Writing has been the thread that allowed her to stitch together the loss of territorial, cultural, linguistic and relational continuity to the complex and confusing experiences that leaving your country brings. She was born in Ponce, Puerto Rico to a "feminist without a tag" and a man "who walked to school without shoes"—her mom and dad. Emma writes to uncover what is hidden. In her writing process, she works in two languages, and whether the product reveals it or not, she crafts words together to reflect the fabric of a bilingual mind and self.

**David R. Surette's** new book of poetry, *Stable*, earned an Honors Award at this year's Massachusetts Book Awards. He is the author of four other collections: *Wicked Hard, The Immaculate Conception Mothers' Club, Young Gentlemen's School* and *Easy to Keep, Hard to Keep In*, which earned Highly Recommended status at the 8th Annual Massachusetts Book Awards. He teaches English and coaches varsity hockey at East Bridgewater High School. He lives on Cape Cod.

**Jeri Theriault**, of French Canadian heritage, grew up in Waterville. Her father's father came to Maine from Quebec in the early 20th century, "No wonder my father spoke French almost exclusively until he went into the Marines at age 18!" Theriault has three chapbooks, the latest of which, *In the Museum of Surrender* won the 2013 Encircle chapbook contest. Her full-length collection *Radost, My Red* was released in July 2016 by Moon Pie Press. Her poems have appeared in numerous journals and anthologies including *The Beloit Poetry Journal, The Atlanta Review, Rhino, The Paterson Literary Review* and *Off the Coast*. A three-time Pushcart Prize nominee and a Fulbright recipient, she holds an MFA from Vermont College of Fine Arts. She lives in South Portland.

**Cindy Veach's** poems have appeared in *Prairie Schooner, Poet Lore, Zone 3, Michigan Quarterly Review, The Journal, North American Review, Off the Coast* and elsewhere and work is forthcoming in *Agni* and *Nimrod*. Her debut poetry collection, *Gloved Against Blood*, is forthcoming from CavanKerry Press (fall 2017). She manages fundraising programs for non-profit organizations and lives in Manchester by the Sea, Massachusetts.

**Robert J. Ward** is a retired high school English teacher who has always lived in Massachusetts. The poem, "Descent Into Harvey," expresses a wish to transcend a geographical boundary. It was inspired by his second trip to Atlantic Canada to delve into family history, but his first time at that particular border crossing.

**Danielle Woerner** is a writer, songwriter, singer, educator, and the co-founder of Sunrise County Arts Institute in Milbridge, ME. Her journalistic work and poetry have been featured in national publications including Newsweek, Classical Singer, and New Music Connoisseur; regional monthlies including Hudson Valley Magazine and Chronogram; and weekly newspapers from the Woodstock (NY) Times to the Machias Valley News Observer. Danielle began writing haiku in earnest in 2012, to cope with "prose burnout" after cranking out a 50,000-word NaNoWriMo novel draft in 30 days. She and her husband, formerly vacationers on the Downeast-Acadia coast, then part-timers in Milbridge for several years, have resided in the town full-time since 2014. Most of her recent haiku are observations of life and nature in Downeast Maine.

**Leslie Wood** is an artist and writer who grew up in Kentucky. She has a Master's degree in art education, and taught art in Kentucky for many years. Since 2002, she has been working with Fredda Paul on a project to preserve, through words, images, and interviews with other tribal members, the fast-disappearing knowledge of healing with native plants. She has been writing Fredda's stories, passed to her through Fredda's oral telling. She is a proud forager of food and medicine, and considers dandelions and goose tongue greens among her favorite foods.

# Acknowledgements

The idea for this book came about ten years ago, when Michael and I moved from Cape Cod to Maine. We fell in love with the "real downeast" beyond Bar Harbor and settled in the tiny town of Robbinston (population 525) on Passamaquoddy Bay. The presence of the Passamaquoddy tribe and Canada close by were appealing. The thought of joining these three sovereign nations in dialogue presented itself early on. It would take much longer to make the book happen.

Michael and I began editing *Off the Coast* literary journal, which we held for eight years before passing it on to a member of the editorial board. I returned to school to earn a degree in Electronic Publishing. Work on the book finally began in the winter of 2016.

This book would not have been possible without the help of Marcus LiBrizzi and Bernie Vinzani, professors at the University of Maine Machias, who all contributed to my education in Book Arts and publishing.

Special thanks to Leslie Wood for serving as amanuensis for Fredda Paul's work, "Eli-kisi-kikuhut Cihpolakon" (How the Eagle Was Healed), and to Robert Leavitt, director of the Mi'kmaq-Maliseet Institute at the University of New Brunswick in Canada, for the Passamaquoddy translations and phonetic spellings (for more information visit the Passamaquoddy-Maliseet Language portal: http://pmportal. org/splash).

Adelene Ellenberg and Michele Leavitt gave invaluable advice on permissions. Josh Bodwell, Executive Director of Maine Writers & Publishers Alliance (MWPA), helped with names and resources. Stephanie Gough and Sarah Murphy helped with connections to Canadian writers and poets. Jim Coogan of Harvest Home Books many years ago gave me confidence in the power of small presses.

A special thank you to Michael R. Brown, as always, for being there lending support and expertise in all things.

And thank you to all of the poets and writers who were willing to share their work, without whom this book would not have been possible.